S0-CDN-771

NO LONGER ALONE

Dorothy Howard

David C. Cook Publishing Co.
ELGIN, ILLINOIS—WESTON, ONTARIO

David C. Cook Publishing Co., Elgin, IL 60120
Printed in the United States of America
Library of Congress Catalog Number: 74-32603
ISBN: 0-912692-60-X

*This book is dedicated
to my daughters,
Priscilla and Deborah*

PREFACE

There are many ways of sharing the Christian life with others. Perhaps the most lasting way is through writing. In this book, I have shared my discoveries in walking in this new way of life. I have written with the hope that someone reading this book will be challenged to try the liberating life found in God and made possible through His love.

As a new Christian, I have been deeply influenced by the counsel and writings of many more mature Christians. I have tried to give credit where it is due to the original donor, but can only say a word of thanks for the thoughts that have been absorbed through much reading and study from the many others who have influenced my life.

I wish to express my appreciation to my friends, Lois Comer and Bertha Elliott, for the valuable assistance they have given me in the mechanics of preparing the manuscript and for their suggestions which have been of great help.

Acknowledgment and thanks are due *Eternity* and *Decision* magazines for the use of two of my articles which have been made a part of the book.

CONTENTS

CHAPTER ONE

In the Beginning

Beside the pleasure derived from acquired knowledge, there lurks in the mind and tinged with a shade of sadness, an unsatisfactory longing for something beyond the present — a striving toward regions yet unknown and unopened.

— *Karl W. Humbolt*

Standing on the deck of the French liner, *Liberte,* I watched the skyline of New York fade out of sight in the gray mist of the early August morning.

This trip was to be a vacation. I had no inkling that it would change the course of my life.

The murky gray pallor hung over the ship and the sea, blending them into one. Most of the passengers had gone inside but I continued to lean on the rail, watching the wake of the ship. It glowed for a few seconds in the fog, then faded into nothingness.

The entire dreary scene was a reflection of my inner thoughts. I was a devotee of a cold, ethical philosophy of humanism with no power except that generated from within myself. Lately, this system of thought was giving little satisfaction. No longer were the achievements I had realized in the business world bringing the happiness they once did. And then this terrible emptiness! Was there a state of being in which one could experience happiness, peace of mind and true fulfillment of life? There was no answering voice to these questions.

A mask of complacency covered the turmoil that existed in my inner self. It served to hide the fears that held me in their grip: fear of what would happen to my children if I failed to make it in life, fear of death, fear of old age and countless other fears.

Enough of this self-introspection. I went inside to join the others in the fun and pleasures of the trip.

It was in Holland that I first experienced a fleeting premonition that something different could happen in my life. Climbing the huge stairway of the Peace Palace in The Hague, I stood for a moment gazing up at the life-sized statue of Christ. The sculptor had caught an expression of strength and tranquillity in the face of Jesus which fascinated me. I paused long enough to read the words inscribed on the base of the statue: "My peace I give unto you. . . ." Was this really true and was there a remote chance I could experience it?

The thought was momentary. I went on to other scenes and places. England was the last stop. Next to the hotel was a bombed-out crater where, perhaps, a beautiful building had once stood. I stared out the window, wondering how it must have felt back there in 1944 to have no place of safety as Hitler's bombs fell all about.

The English hostess at the hotel had joined me as I stood gazing at the open crater.

"Don't you find yourself still hating those who did this to your country?" I questioned.

She looked at me for a moment and replied, "No, not now. At first I did. But spending night after night in the dark, cold shelters, I had to acquire a faith in

14

a Power greater than myself or go berserk. I learned to pray, as many did. God became real to me. I found that hatred had to go if I were to have peace within myself."

Amazing!

As I walked away, a strange longing tugged at me — a longing for some kind of faith in someone greater than myself that would bring meaning to life. Perhaps there might be Someone beyond this present existence who cares? How could one know?

Sometime later, after my return to the States, a religious book was given me to read. I looked at it with distaste for I had little use for religion as such. The book was placed in an inconspicuous spot on the bookshelf and promptly forgotten.

Several weeks later my friend called. Did I enjoy the book? I had to confess that I hadn't read it yet but promised to start that evening. Since I didn't want to hurt her, I decided the easiest way out was to read the story and erase it from my mind.

From the start the author challenged me with her adventure of discovering God. She maintained that God could be known personally through Jesus Christ, for He came to this world to show us what God was really like.

She pointed out that whatever the outward and inward hungers of the human heart, there is a basic hunger in all humanity to know God even though it may be unrecognized. I had that hunger but I didn't want to admit it. The book closed with this invitation: "I will certainly not cast out anyone who comes to Me."

15

After I finished reading the book my first reaction was the impossibility of the whole idea. How could a person discover a faith in something he neither believed in nor cared to believe in? I was willing to admit to the manifestations of a Power that held the universe together. As to Jesus Christ, to me He was some ethereal figure who had lived some two thousand years ago and was considered a great teacher by some. I wished I had not read the book. It was too disturbing.

Weeks passed and the author's challenge continued to haunt me. There was an intense struggle going on within my inner being. Coming in from a New Year's Eve get-together, I sat in a chair for some time. Thinking over the past year, I wondered if the year ahead would be as devoid of meaning as the past year.

Finally, in desperation, I knelt and said, "Here I am, God. I don't know this Christ and have little faith in Him. But if He is real, help me to discover Him and know You."

This was the first real prayer I had ever made in my life and it came from the depths of a very empty soul.

As I continued kneeling there in the silence, a deep peace and quietness permeated my whole being. I felt strangely clean, and oh, so much loved. This Stranger had given me a new identity and a sense of wholeness. There was no visible presence, but in some unexplainable way, I knew for a certainty that God is real. I had found Him through the reality of Jesus Christ.

I went to bed that early morning with the assurance that my prayer for help had somehow placed a key in my hands — a key that would unlock the door to a way of life previously unknown if I would dare to accept the adventure offered to me.

CHAPTER TWO

Was It a Dream?

If we are but fixed and resolute — bent on high and holy ends, we shall find means to them on every side and at every moment; and even obstacles and opposition will but make us "like the fabled spectre-ships, which sail the fastest in the very teeth of the wind."

— *Tryon Edwards*

My first waking thought the next morning was, had I dreamed the experience of the previous night? Had it been a figment of my imagination or was it here to stay? What would my friends think if I should tell them?

Until the night before, my life had been centered in the pursuit of the cult of humanism. A number of us had been devotees of humanism, which is faith in the supreme value and self-perfectibility of the human personality. The goal is the production of a free society in which all people cooperate for the common good. It is a system of thought and action concerned only with human interests. Its power centers solely in the individual. After all, the only real and tangible things in life are those that can be experienced through the five senses — so I thought. Previously I had felt no need to bring a Supreme Being into my world of thought and action.

Even now it was difficult to admit something had really happened to me that defied the once logical explanations of the materialistic concepts of life I had held as the truth. It was not easy to admit that I had been trapped in the empty wasteland of my own controlled world. I had played god over my aims, my thoughts, my acts, my daily life. In a moment's time, this control had changed hands. It was now God's turn.

I was challenged with the possibility of a dimension in human personality that is not solely explainable on scientific evidence, that the psyche cannot reach its fulfillment until God enters in and becomes merged with it.

Some might call this experience conversion; some might call it commitment. I only know that Christ stepped out of history and became reality in my life. It happened in a strange and incomprehensible way and in a moment's time.

There was no verbal explanation that could be given for this peace that still remained from the previous night's adventure in prayer. Nor could I explain how the emptiness, that had once been a part of my life, had really gone. This was no imagination but strong reality.

Added to these changes was the very personal experience of having met a Friend for the first time. I could not escape the awareness of His presence. This realization of God's love aroused an inexpressible yearning to know Him better.

Just how does one go about knowing God? I know of no set rules and there is no special road map marking the way. It must be an individual experiment in faith. I was not quite sure where to begin or where it would take me.

In the oil business plant, where I was working at the time, we had a very modern laboratory. Various formulas were created and tested to meet the new trends in industrial manufacturing. The chief chemist worked out various phases of the formulas through daily small experiments. These were finalized into a written formula and given to the blender. He would then begin production of the lubricant. To be successful, the recipe must be mixed accurately, with no deviations.

A young blender trainee, fresh from college, decided on his own to make one minor change in the formula he was producing by substituting another chemical for the one specified. This resulted in an explosion. The material became a useless mess, nothing like the master chemist had intended.

The concepts and principles of this new way of life I had accepted must have been worked out in the laboratory of God. They should be workable in life here on earth. Would I find them workable for me?

The reasonable thing to do, if I wanted to find out if God could be known to some degree and if this new way of life was really workable in my present existence, would be to follow some formula.

Did the Bible contain the needed information somewhere within its covers? On occasion, I had opened the Bible, only to have found it dull and unreadable. Perhaps what had happened to me would change the dullness.

Then, too, if I could talk to God as I did the night I met Him, some communication might be established. This would take some faith on my part.

This new resolution to start reading the Bible and praying involved an initial risk. I would be staking everything on what had not as yet been proved in my experience. But then, I had always thought of life as a risk. In fact, it might be said that we are able to live only to the extent that we are able to risk. I reasoned there would be nothing to lose and everything to gain.

I must dare to try the experiment of reading the Bible and praying to God. Had I known what the future held for me because of this resolution, I might have wavered in my determination.

CHAPTER THREE

God Loves!

Love is the greatest thing that God can give us, for he himself is love; and it is the greatest thing we can give to God, for it will also give ourselves, and carry with it all that is ours. The apostle calls it the bond of perfection; it is the old, the new, and the great commandment, and all the commandments, for it is the fulfilling of the law. It does the work of all the other graces without any instrument but its own immediate virtue.

— *Jeremy Taylor*

THE NEXT MORNING, sleepily remembering my new resolution, I reached for the New Testament on my night table. Leafing through the pages, I was struck by the beauty of the opening words of the Gospel of John. I read on for several chapters and the dullness I had anticipated was not there. The words came alive.

There came a realization that for some utterly inexplicable reason God had found something lovable in all of us. The love of God is one of the greatest realities of the universe. It is a very personal and intimate thing. These words were written for each individual and God seemed to be speaking to me through them: "For God loved the world so much that he gave his only Son so that anyone who believes in him shall not perish but have eternal life. God did not send his Son into the world to condemn it, but to save it" (John 3:16,17, The Living Bible).

I had been met by One who knew me as I was, yet loved me and cared for me just the same. This love is wonderful and without comparison. To one reared from childhood in an orthodox or fundamentalist background, it might be difficult to understand the excitement of my discovery. As I gaze up at the stars, the moon and the sun, realizing the power behind this orderly creation, I am awed at the thought of this God who could love and care so much for each tiny part of His creation.

In one of his sermons Sam Shoemaker said he thought very likely God's last words to Jesus before sending Him to earth were, "Give them all My love."

God's love to us is the source of our love to others. His love is nonpossessive and is not conditioned by the recipient, but full-flowing. He continues to love us regardless of the manner in which we receive His love. God is infinitely patient with us and believes in us when we have lost faith in ourselves. How patient He is with us at the slow steps we take in living this new life under His direction, our mistakes and failures. Yet He continues to love us.

I experienced a growing conviction, which keeps deepening as time goes on, that not God's love alone but His power, too, is immeasurable and even awesome. As we come into relationship with Him, He offers us this power to live an abundant life. Yet so many of us continue to search for life in other directions. God's grace toward us is patient and more persistent than even our sinfulness toward Him.

Looking back over the circumstances leading to my commitment, I saw how God had patiently pursued me. In fact He had done everything possible to bring me to Him.

The trip, the book, the disturbing thoughts over

the emptiness of life had all been part of the plan of the loving God. Then came the groping for a reality that seemed beyond reach, consumated in the night I met Him. God pursues us in many ways, giving us every possible chance to meet and know Him.

I continued to read the New Testament, finding new perspectives for my life. As I read about Christ and His teachings, I found Him to be a very disturbing Person. He was awakening in me a realization that there is such a thing as sin which, up to now, I had not faced. I had previously considered sin as mistakes made and common to everyone. The way to take care of them had been to "sweep them under the rug" and forget about them. In doing this it was little wonder that there was such restlessness and emptiness to life. God was challenging me with His love, to share everything with Him, seeking forgiveness for the sins in my life, and to begin this new life with Him.

From His recorded teachings, I felt a hunger to be a better person. I could not meet this Christ and go on my way exactly as I had. This confrontation was no transitory experience but a challenge to be a reproducer of His ways. I wanted to live my life after the pattern of His. I wondered whether it could be done.

I read and reread the Gospels. Jesus was the central figure and an elusive picture began to emerge. The writers portrayed Him as a real person, an understanding person. The great love and care He constantly showed to others while here on earth fascinated me. I began to see what God is like through this man called Jesus. His love reached out through the written pages to me. I had an intensive yearning to become better acquainted with Him, and to be a reproducer of His ways.

Many times I have been asked, "How can you believe in God when you can't see Him, talk to Him in person or even touch Him?" Love cannot be touched. I love my children deeply but I cannot touch that emotion called love. I just know that it is there. This I have discovered in my relationship with God. I just know that He is there because of His love for me as a person who has found Him in this new way of life.

> If Jesus Christ is a man,
> And only a man — I say
> That of all mankind I cleave to Him
> And to Him will I cleave alway.
>
> If Jesus Christ is a God,
> And the only God — I swear
> I will follow Him through heaven and hell
> The earth, the sea, the air.
> — RICHARD WATSON GILDER

There are many things in the New Testament which I did not understand, and still do not understand. However, I am convinced that within its pages is the formula for a full and satisfying life to be lived in the now of our existence.

Christ's ethical teachings on various matters opened up new vistas of living. He never seemed to lay down rules. What He tried to teach us were principles. That is why His way of life is so vital and free. Rules tend to become obsolete. The principles of Christ are eternal. In applying a principle of His in a certain circumstance, I have discovered that this same principle may be applied quite differently in differing situations.

The realities of the Bible have taught me the art of living in two worlds at the same time — the material world and the inner world. People are portrayed just as they are, with their faults and failures as well as their victories. Yet God continued to love them. I felt a kinship to them.

God must love us tremendously to have sent His Son to us that we might become acquainted with Him.

CHAPTER FOUR

"Trust Me"

We trust as we love, and where we love. If we love Christ much, surely we shall trust Him much.

— Thomas Brooks

In MY SEARCH FOR GOD, I read several books on the historic creeds of the Church. They stirred no answering response within me. I was continually driven back, again and again, to the study and reading of the New Testament.

The words of Jesus, "I am the way" haunted me. They confronted me with a Lord seen and known to be a man but who acted and taught with all the authority of God Himself. I determined to seek Him through every available avenue.

Christ asks three things of us: love, faith and obedience. The formula appears simple enough. If we love a person, we have faith in that person. Christ challenges us, in our love for Him, to trust in His integrity, strength and ability to take care of us. This trust implies an instinctive unquestioning belief in this Person no matter what happens. Little did I realize how costly it would become as I traveled along this way.

Either an intimate walk with God is possible, leading to a full and productive life, or it is not workable in the now of our existence. This I had to know.

My childhood was spent on a farm. I can remember the day when, walking with my dad, we came to a small turbulent stream which had to be crossed. My father started walking over on the rocks ahead of me, calling me to follow. Partway across, he looked around to be sure I was all right. He was surprised to find me still sitting on the bank of the stream.

He came back and said, "Take my hand and let's walk over together." I gave another look at the rushing brook. It looked even more impossible and frightening. I shook my head, refusing to leave my safe spot.

Dad sat down beside me and took my hand. He said, "You know that I love you, don't you? And I know that you love me. So why don't you trust me? I promise not to let go of your hand."

Clinging to his hand, I got up and we started over the rocks. Because of his expression of love, I had a child's faith to really believe that nothing could happen to me and dared to follow my father's command.

Jesus seemed to be asking the same simple trust from me now.

There is a world of meaning in these two words, "I believe." Science demands that we deal with facts, not with dreams and imaginings. The first law of science is that if there is evidence for a thing, it must be put to the test.

Problems and difficulties in life are common to all. I had enough naive realism to believe that there would be continuing problems and hardships to be faced even though I had started in a new way of life. In times past, I had brought to bear against these difficulties all the force and power I could, all the struggling and resisting of which I had been capable. At times I could meet them with some sort of solution. What difference would my newfound faith make?

There was a challenge in the words of Jesus, "Anything is possible if you have faith" (Mark 9:23, TLB). This faith isn't some general "Pollyanna" kind of faith; it is faith in depth. It doesn't come easy to believe. It is a struggle many times. Nor does it descend on us in a showerlike covering. Instead, Jesus describes it as a grain of mustard seed that can grow into great proportions.

Starting with the solid fact of my first personal experience when I accepted Christ, a seed of faith was planted and the experiment had commenced. I am discovering there is trust in the idea that faith is that quality or power by which the things desired become the things possessed. Faith shatters and breaks apart the problems or difficulties. It helps me to see all the elements of the problem but doesn't stop there. The possibility of a solution emerges. It may not be the one I had thought possible but could be an entirely new approach. Christ keeps inciting me to this life of adventure, experiment, and discovery, patiently teaching me that faith is indeed a gift from God. I find I am nearest to the possession of faith when I realize my own helplessness and complete dependence upon God, for He is GOD.

Somewhere I read that real faith is not that we keep our minds on God every minute, but that we have finally caught the idea that God never allows His mind to wander for one second from us.

My belief in Christ deepens by the facts of my own experience, facts that are unanswerable and indisputable.

One day I was rushed to the hospital for surgery and a biopsy which might mean cancer. I was filled with fear and dread, alone and afraid. Then these words came, "I will keep you in perfect peace if your mind is stayed on me."

I focused my thoughts on God. An unbelievable calm and peace surged through me. I enjoyed a good night's rest without medication. The next morning I faced surgery with a calmness that was not my own. God had given me the faith to believe that I was not alone in this situation. He was with me no matter what the outcome.

There are times of doubting, especially when things do not turn out the way I believe they should. When these doubts take over, Jesus dares me to believe in Him because of His works. The God whose power holds the planets in their orbit, who provides the warmth of the sun and the cool of the night, surely may be trusted to take over the operation of one little life.

"Believe" is a word of action. It instills faith that brings healing, not only to me, but to others. Christ did not lay down rules that became obsolete with passing generations. He taught principles that are applicable to everyday living. It takes an act of faith, sometimes, to apply the principle of love to a difficult situation.

My employer stopped me one morning and asked me to talk with one of the men in the factory. Joe was an excellent worker and was really needed in the plant as he possessed special skills for this type of job.

However, he was thoroughly disliked by everyone who was obliged to be near him or work with him. Joe was disruptive, vindictive, and a real troublemaker. I had little faith in my ability to cope with the problem but promised to do what I could to ease the situation.

Early the next morning, I called Joe to come into my office. He knocked on my door. Opening it, I motioned him toward the chair by my desk, at the same time silently asking for some help from God.

As I sat looking at this man, my first question was, "Why do you do these things, Joe, when you know that it will eventually mean the loss of your job unless you mend your ways?"

Joe looked at me beligerently and replied, "I have no friends and everyone hates me." He continued to spit out the hatred and dislike for his fellow workers. He finally came to a stop. Looking at me, he said, "So what are you going to do about it?"

My first impulse was to recommend his immediate dismissal. It seemed impossible to believe there could be any change in his life. Then came an inner thought of trying an experiment of faith. I wondered what would happen if I tried applying God's love and sensitivity to this situation.

I looked at Joe and said, "I want to be your friend, Joe." This took him by surprise and he muttered, "You must be nuts, lady."

He was to report to me every Tuesday morning at ten o'clock and we would just talk things over. Meanwhile, his part was to attempt to get along with his fellow workers. Joe walked out of the office in a daze. I sat there wondering if I had taken leave of my senses after reviewing our conversation.

For the next six weeks, each Tuesday morning found Joe waiting at my door. Each week it was the same old story. Gripes and more gripes was all he managed to talk about. My faith in the power of love over situations was fast waning. The seventh week Joe came in and there was a real change in his attitude. Even before he spoke I knew something had happened. He told me his fellow workers had changed and were being kind to him. Things were going great. Two of the men had become his buddies. Joe is still working in the same place and is now liked and respected by his fellow workers.

From this situation I learned the concrete fact that faith in God and the power of His love can change situations and people. He asks only that I dare to accept the challenge and put faith to work. There are times I have failed God wretchedly in this area of obedience. Yet He still dares to trust me and love me. Through each act of obedience in faith, God becomes increasingly real to me.

Faith is not an odd peculiarity of religion only. It is the hub on which our everyday life turns. We awaken in the morning and step out in faith that the transportation facility will get us to our job. Sometimes it breaks down, but we don't lose our faith in it. We eat our daily food in the belief that it is essential to life. We accept people in faith that they will not let us down. Almost everything we do daily reflects a certain amount of faith on our part. Yet we are dubious about having faith in God.

This newfound faith does answer many of the questions and inward longings of the soul. It produces a chain reaction in life. Faith in God produces a love and service toward my fellowman. The mass of humanity becomes individualistic and God asks that I become involved with their needs. Unless I do, my faith is in vain.

One evening last summer I walked along the beach on Cape Cod, watching the fog roll in from the sea. It was very quiet for the beach was deserted. Before I realized it, the mist was so dense that all objects were obliterated. I had stayed too long. Because of the heavy fog, I lost my sense of direction. It was impossible to find my way back to the cabin where I was staying with my friend, Marie. Panic and fear enveloped me as I stood there wondering what to do. Then I heard a voice calling in the mist. I answered and continued answering until my friend emerged from the murky gray darkness and together we walked home.

One night, in the mists of doubt, theory and humanism, God heard my cry for help and answered it. He has become a very real Person to whom I have given my love and allegiance.

CHAPTER FIVE

Experiment in Prayer

Prayer is not eloquence, but earnestness; not the definition of helplessness but the feeling of it; not figures of speech, but earnestness of soul.

— *Hannah More*

PRAYER MAKES CHILDREN of us all and no responsible adult wants to appear childish. For this, and
other reasons, prayer was a luxury item I rarely used.
It was reserved for cases of disaster or dire need.

God heard my prayer that New Year's Eve and
had assured me of His love. I didn't want to lose
this friendship. Prayer, talking with God, seemed to
be the means of cementing our relationship.

Through the experiment of personal prayer, I discovered, and am still discovering, its great potential.
It creates an openness in which self passes out of the
door into a divine encounter. It is more than petition;
it is self-surrender to God.

However, nothing which enriches and empowers
life ever just happens. A price must be paid. If I
wanted to become acquainted with God, I had to set
aside a specific time daily to pray. The early morning hour seemed to be the time with the fewest interruptions.

From the outset, there was an awareness that the
very physical conditions of existence connive to make

solitude almost impossible. It was difficult to shut the doors of my mind against the insistent intrusion of the outside world. Fire engines racing through the streets with sirens blasting; garbage men arguing over their work; the ring of the telephone and countless other interruptions made me think this was going to be an impossible experiment. Along with the outside intrusions were the wandering thoughts dancing through my mind at the wrong time. It took real discipline to concentrate on the fact that this was the time I had set apart to talk with God.

At first, all I could manage was a sentence prayer. Then there were mornings when the sky seemed to have a leaden covering between God and me. I was certain that He was not listening, for my words bounced back at me like a rubber ball. These were discouraging times. Through these dull experiences in prayer there came a glimmer of faith to believe that, even though I felt nothing, God was still there.

During my early teen years, when I attended church for a short period of time, I often wondered if God was really listening to us when we prayed. It seemed that prayer was a formality to be observed. Now I was discovering my own problems with this communication medium with God.

Often I found myself going through the motions of praying the same time each day because it was the proper thing to do, saying the same words because it was expected of a person who claimed a relationship with God. Prayer was becoming a meaningless form to me.

To overcome this, I began to picture myself having a lively conversation with a friend. I shared various things that had happened during the past twenty-four hours: my joys, my activities, my problems. Through this new approach, God did become more real. I felt that He was really listening and this made prayer something to look forward to in spite of the occasional leaden times and times of distraction.

God is a disturbing Person to meet. In His presence, I feel that no secrets are hidden. The inner me is revealed in its nakedness, stripped of every disguise. Until that night I met Him, I had never thought of myself as either good or bad. "Sin" was not a word in my vocabulary and had little or no meaning. Anything I did which might have been considered bad, I had chalked off as merely an error.

There were many things not exactly right in my life, needing confession and change. I began to wonder what had happened to all my "goodness." It was not easy for me to acknowledge to an unseen Presence the failure I made of running my life in my own way. It was embarrassing to admit to the bitterness I felt towards a person who had wronged me. Harder still, to admit that perhaps some of the fault lay in me. But again and again, I can come into God's presence, making confession freely and fully, finding the forgiveness I need. During these times I come face to face with an overwhelming love — the love of the Son of God.

Although I am not a mystic, there are times when I have felt God's presence in wordless communion. There has been communication between us with un-uttered petitions and without a spoken word, an interchange of thoughts. It is during the time of silence that God does have a chance to speak to the inner self. It is then that the experience of personal prayer becomes the burning center of life.

In my reading of the Gospels, I realized that Jesus constantly sought renewal of life in solitary prayer with the Father. This was the great priority of His life. It was the aloneness of His private prayer life that gave Him the tremendous faith in His Father — the strong motivation of His every word and deed. It is this faith that has challenged Christians down through the ages. I am convinced that if Jesus felt such constant need of communion with the Father, how much more I need it.

Prayer, solely for self, becomes a stagnant thing. God is also interested in caring for the needs of others, and prayer becomes the means through which miracles are performed. Not only are others helped in times of decision and crises through our prayers, but we, too, have our faith renewed.

A friend of mine was having a difficult time with her marriage. My prayer was at first perfunctory — somewhat like this, "God, please bless Mary, she needs it." Gradually a burden of prayer settled upon me. I started to talk earnestly with God about the situation. I didn't admit to Mary that I was praying about this in case God might not do anything about it for her. Then we would both have felt let down. Faith is difficult for those whose sole power has centered in their ability to make things happen if possible.

After a month of daily prayer for Mary, I happened to meet her on the street. Her face glowed with happiness. I asked her what had happened to make her so joyous. With a smile, she answered, "Things are taking a turn for the better in our marriage. It is like a miracle."

Looking at her in open-mouth astonishment, I blurted out, "Then God does hear prayer after all." She looked at me puzzled and I had to tell her what I had been doing. I confessed I had hoped, but really wasn't sure, that God would do anything. It was difficult to admit my lack of faith to another person. This confession of failure drew us closer together and she was able to admit to the same failure.

This was my first answer to prayer for another person, a real tangible answer. It did much to strengthen my faith in God.

As time passes I am discovering that not all prayers I have requested have been answered. There have been prayers for loved ones for healing, only to have them die. Why? There is no pat answer.

God's delay in answering our prayers often causes bewilderment and grief. But the delays and the silences of God have to be experienced and trusted if faith is to grow.

In the growing relationship with God through prayer experiences and through reading the Bible, I have become convinced that God loves us. Because of this love, I believe that God hears our anguished cries. At times that is hard to believe, particularly when we are so hemmed in by problems, so desperately in need of help that we even wonder if God exists. He does, and He cares. In ways unknown to us, He answers every prayer. It may not be in the expected way but there is always an answer. At times the answer may be, "No, not now" or even a flat "no." This is not easy to accept.

Through my prayer experiences, I have discovered that I need to get past the accepted formalities to an open vision of God. This means coming to a sure knowledge that, no matter what we feel or see, we are in His presence. He is listening and responding in actions seen and unseen.

What really matters is that in this fast-paced life I make a place to be alone for daily conversation with God. Without this time of communion, life loses a dimension, both for myself and for others. The practice of prayer affirms God's promises, and lives are changed; situations are changed; miracles happen in others as well as to myself.

At first, I thought of prayer as a once-a-day routine to be observed regardless of feelings or circumstances. Now I am discovering the adventure of prayer. It is a conversation with God. After finishing my time of prayer, God is not left there in the room but is with me throughout the day. It took some time for me to realize this and what a discovery!

In the realm of relationships, we enjoy talking over the day's joys as well as problems with our friends and loved ones. We are grateful for the gifts bestowed on us and try in many ways to thank the giver and let this person know how much it is appreciated. If there is something that happens to us not to our liking, we do not lose any time in letting the person know exactly what we think about it. This is life. Communication is the means of cementing deep and personal relationships.

Prayer is talking with God. It need not be confined to a certain time of day but can become a joyous means of knowing Him. One morning while walking to work, I thought of how good it was just to be alive and well. The sky was an intense blue and the air was crisp. Without thinking I breathed a prayer of thanks to God for the joy of it all. Somehow He seemed so close and this was the beginning of times of spontaneous conversation with Him.

Then there are times when life crushes in on us with some problem impossible to solve. There comes a release when it is shared with God. I have found that I don't need to wait until the set time of day to have this communication.

There are times when I do not like what is happening in my life and there is a growing freedom to let God know about it. Things may not change but through this medium of prayer I can find release.

I am discovering that God is fingertip close and prayer has become a way of life.

CHAPTER SIX

Loving in a New Way

Love is an image of God, and not a lifeless image, but the living essence of the divine nature which beams full of all goodness.

— *Martin Luther*

THERE HAVE BEEN MANY BOOKS written about man. Is he primarily a rational being or an emotional being? Great scholars have come to the conclusion that he is primarily an emotional being.

As human beings we are capable of expressing joy or sorrow; hope or dismay; love or hate. Jesus took the primary emotion, love, and demanded that we love Him with all our heart, soul, and mind, and that we love our neighbor as ourself.

In life, we set goals for ourselves which we strive to attain. This love is God's objective and is not finalized in one act in time. It starts with a commitment to Jesus Christ when God implants this new way of loving, His gift to us. Just as a seedling grows into a tree over a period of time, so does love. It is an experimental, growing process, requiring great disciplines.

Jesus wanted us to be sure to realize the importance of our complete involvement. He used the words, "with . . . heart, soul, and mind" (Matthew 22:37, TLB). This love process takes over the intellect as well as the emotions so that there will be a oneness of purpose.

Until now, I had thought of the Christian mode of life to be an intolerable, dull and boring affair, entered into only by those who wanted to live a monastic existence. It seemed to be a repression of everything I wanted to be or to do. Was this the way I would have to live my life if I were to continue as a Christian?

To my surprise and amazement I find it isn't so. As I give these loves of life over to God — my job, my home, my friends, my plans, my pleasures and my ambitions — He gives them back to me richly blessed by His presence. I am finding the Christian way of life to be an abundant way of life. It is a happy life, adventurous, exciting and full of purpose in spite of the sorrows and disappointments that fall across my path. Learning to give these priorities of love to God is showing me that the spiritual world is a real world after all. It is involvement in the present life, a living in a new dimension in our same world.

When God invades our hearts, there is a paradox. We are torn loose from earthly attachments and ambitions. At the same time, we discover that God hurls the same world back into our hearts. Only this time it is seen through God's eyes and touched with His love and compassion.

No one succeeds in keeping the whole law. To love as God wants takes a lifetime of learning. However, each triumph is like a silver thread woven in a tapestry by a master craftsman. Someday it will be finalized in a picture of beauty when we come face to face with Christ. The hallmark of the Christian is a quality of life — love — the product of the Holy Spirit. No two lives are ever alike in its expression.

CHAPTER SEVEN

Surrender

In the many adversities and trials of life it is often hard to say "Thy will be done." But why not say it? God ever does only what is right and wise and best; what is prompted by a father's love, and what to his children will work out their highest good.

— *Edward Payson*

WHEN I SURRENDERED ALL that I knew of myself to all that I knew of Christ, I had made a start. I have discovered since then that surrender is not a one-time deal. It is a continuous process. Surrender is a willingness to stop managing my own life and to let God take it over. It is a willingness to say with Jesus, "Not my will, . . . but your will be done" (Luke 22:42, Today's English Version).

The aim is not my personal goodness but a moment-by-moment joyous instant obedience to God's will. However, sometimes I obey and sometimes not.

When I get into a tough situation, I begin to think of how God also has to surrender as He sets us free to do what we want to do and let us take the consequences of our choice. Again and again, He would like to take us into those everlasting arms, hold us close and shield us from our mistakes, but we are unwilling to come to Him. So God stands silently by and loves us and waits until we give Him that thing or that person we hold so dear.

During the first few months of living in this new relationship with God, I felt I had it made. Life was going along fairly well. As far as I knew, I had surrendered everything to God, that is, all except my job. I was quite sure that He was not particularly interested in that anyhow. I needed it to continue to live and support my children, so why make an issue of it.

I attended a conference where various speakers challenged us with the idea of being willing to yield ourselves to new ideas, new methods, new goals. One particular speaker asked us to be willing to take the risk of changing jobs.

The idea of surrendering my job to God made me very uneasy. I knew that I still controlled this area. Until now, I had been unwilling to surrender the job because I was afraid God might want me to enter the religious field. This wasn't for me! I had worked too hard to get where I was in the business world and I wasn't planning to give it up at this stage.

This particular conference lasted for four days. The whole emphasis was on being willing to take a risk in various areas. God seemed to be challenging me to take the risk of giving my job to Him. I knew there would be no real or lasting peace unless I made this surrender.

Early one afternoon I went off by myself and sat under a tree to think it over. Somewhat reluctantly I placed my job in God's hands with the proviso, "no missionary work and no religious work." Still no peace. Finally I came to the point where I prayed, "All right, God. You win. I want You more than the job, more than anything else in this world, so take it."

A deep peace settled through my being.

Returning home I soon forgot about the surrender I had made. Three months later a telephone call came from New York, asking me to consider a position as business manager for a religious organization.

I didn't want to live in New York. I really didn't want to leave my good position. Nor did I want to leave my friends. Above all, I didn't want to work for a religious organization.

I had forgotten my promise to God that He could have my job and I would do as He wished. However, God had not forgotten.

The New York firm asked me to come and at least look the position over before making a final decision. I came to the city and was impressed with their magazine, their work and the people I met, but I went home telling myself that it wasn't the job for me. The firm gave me four weeks to make a decision, asking me to think it over carefully and to pray about it. This praying about a job was a new experience for me.

This decision was going to change my whole life situation, physically, mentally and spiritually. I wanted to be very sure before I took a leap into this seeming darkness.

I thought perhaps an experiment would help me make the decision. I asked God for something unusual to happen — something really out of the ordinary — so I would be certain that my decision was right. I wanted this experiment to be a direct confirmation and I even set a date for it to happen.

I thought this would be too impossible to happen and would warrant the cancellation of the whole idea.

The specific day arrived. I received a letter in the mail from an unknown publishing house. In the envelope was a single sheet of paper. On it was printed a poem, "Obedience," that covered every objection I had to the new position. It read like this:

I said, "Let me walk in the field,"
He said, "Nay, walk in the town."
I said, "There are no flowers there,"
He said, "No flowers, but a crown."

I said, "But the air is thick,
And fogs are veiling the sun."
He said, "Yet souls are sick,
And souls in the dark are undone."

I said, "But the skies are black,
There is nothing but noise and din."
He wept as He sent me back,
"There is more," He said, "there is sin."

I said, "I shall miss the light,
And friends will miss me, they say."
He said, "Choose you tonight,
If I am to miss you or they."

I pleaded for time to be given,
He said, "Is it hard to decide?
It will not seem hard in Heaven
To have followed the steps of your Guide."

I cast one look on the field,
Then turned my face to the town.
He said, "My child, do you yield?
Will you leave the flowers for a crown?"

Then into His hand went mine
And into my heart came He;
And I walk by a light divine
The path I had feared to see.

Obedience — GEORGE MACDONALD

Although many things have happened which at times have tried my faith in God to the uttermost, I know I am in the spot that God has planned for me.

This commitment unlocked the door to a life of joy and adventure. I am continually making the discovery that God's way of life does produce peace, joy, happiness and a sense of well-being.

CHAPTER EIGHT

Facing Worry, Fear and Anxiety

When we borrow trouble, and look forward into the future and see what storms are coming, and distress ourselves before they come, as to how we shall avert them if they ever do come, we lose our proper trustfulness in God. When we torment ourselves with imaginary dangers, or trials or reverses, we have already parted with that perfect love which casteth out fear.

— *Henry Ward Beecher*

THE CHALLENGE THAT JESUS GAVE, "If you love me, keep my commandments," caused me to wonder what it was He really wanted of me.

Retracing my initial reading of the Gospels, I listed the attributes of those who kept God's commandments. Love, joy, peace, long-suffering, humbleness were some of them. At least these were expected expressions.

I tried to put them into practice, one at a time. What I accomplished one day, I failed on the next. I could be loving for a short time, to everyone — until an obnoxious person crossed my path. Then love was pushed aside momentarily.

It was easy to be joyful when life was going well. But when adversity crossed my path, joy departed. I could live at peace with my fellow workers until they stepped on my toes, then followed a war of words. I was long-suffering to a certain extent, but not for too long a period of time.

The kind of life which God seemed to want of us just didn't fit into the pattern of everyday human living here on earth. I began to wonder if God's way of life was really workable on this planet.

As the attributes of this way of life seemed impossible to practice most of the time, I thought that perhaps if I switched over to the elimination of some of the negatives from my life, things might progress better.

Among the other things listed in the Bible which God did not condone were: hatred, lying, cheating, fearfulness, lack of faith, pride, covetousness and so on.

Through my prayer life there had become an acute awareness of sin. This had not bothered me too much under my previous philosophy. In the natural world one cannot truly appreciate light unless he has experienced darkness. The light that I had discovered was that God exists, that He loves and cares for us. His primary interest is that we may find the joy of life lived under His direction. In this light, I also discovered that sin does exist. It is succumbing to sin that drags us down and pulls us away from God. Until now, I had not faced this fact.

Determined to show my obedience to God, I would take one of the listed sins applicable to myself and try to eliminate it from my life. What I succeeded to accomplish one day would crop out the next. I became utterly discouraged.

Gradually I discovered that my do-it-yourself project was the wrong approach. This way of life was only possible in uniting my life with God. My part was to yield to Him and to love Him. He would help me with the sins that come so naturally to all of us. I have to build on Christ's love for me rather than my love for Him which so often fails and grows tepid and unstable.

God promised me the power to live His life-style through the presence and help of the Holy Spirit. This power would enable me, at times, to do what seemed impossible, to face the many difficulties with a strength not of my own, to become the person God had planned for me to be. My part was involvement.

Worry, fear and anxiety constitute the most devastating enemy of human well-being. If a worry thought is allowed to continuously trickle across the mind, it will ultimately dig a trench. This will grow deeper and will fill with all sorts of anxieties and fears. If allowed to remain they will overpower us.

There is a fascinating spot in Bar Harbor, Maine that I visited a few years ago. The site is on the shoreline and the natives call it "Thunderhole." It is a trench carved deep into the rock formation. It started long ago with a small but constant trickle of sand and surf against the huge rock structure. The continuous beating of the tides carved out a deep hollow. Now at high tide the water pounds into this crevice with a roar like thunder. Worry works the same way, eating its course into our being until it leaves deep trenches in the mind from which there seems to be no escape.

If we will examine our worries we will discover that most of the things we worry about will never happen. We let our thoughts and imaginations run away until the thing we worry about assumes gigantic proportions.

We worry about decisions that have been made. We are very concerned whether we did the right thing. I am learning that any decision once made and consummated has passed into the yesterday of time and cannot be altered. Therefore, the thing to do is to accept it, make the best of it but stop worrying.

The expression, "I am worried sick over this," has often been used by many of us. There is truth in it. If we let worry consume us, we can actually become ill from it. The thing to do to overcome worry is to face it with a frontal attack and determine, with God's help, that it is not going to overcome us. This promise from the Bible has helped me so much in my own worry situations: "Casting all your care upon him; for he careth for you" (I Peter 5:7).

Fear seems to be one of the predominant emotions in everyone. Psychologists state that a baby has but two normal fears: the fear of falling and the fear of noise. All other fears are acquired throughout our lives.

Fear of losing our material possessions, fear of death, fear of the future, fear of our status in society, fear of sickness, and countless other fears are gradually absorbed into our systems. They multiply until they become so great that they rob us of our health and happiness.

Fear is being afraid, a feeling of dread, or anxiety. When it absorbs us it produces a darkness in life. We are held in its bondage and are no longer free to live the life God has planned for us — a life that is joyous and unafraid.

We live in a day when people are afraid of so many things. Jesus was keenly aware of this problem which is common to all men. He keeps repeating these words, "Fear not," and with this reassurance comes the promise that if we will let Him, He will always be with us. Then there is nothing to fear.

Some fears are shadowy and elusive.

I discovered this while on a camping trip with some of my friends. They had to go into town for supplies and left me in charge of the camp. Night came. A storm was approaching and they had not returned. Everything about me was shrouded in inky blackness. I became very fearful. I was alone in a secluded area far from people. I began to think of all the things that might happen. There were so many stories in the news of people being killed all over the country and I was sure I remembered one about a camper.

I let this fear master me. It grew gradually in degree to dread and deep anxiety then to terror. I was certain that someone was out there in the darkness just waiting to kill me. Fear controlled me. I had forgotten that God was there with me.

Unable to cope with the terror that was engulfing me, I was so frightened I cried out to God to help me. As if to reassure me that He was there and that there was nothing to fear, there was a flash of lightning. Then another and another. Everything stood out in the naked brilliance and I saw nothing to alarm me. All the scary things had disappeared.

Shortly afterwards my friends returned from the trip to town and all was well. This experience taught me to let God take over when these shadowy fears creep into my mind.

Another way to overcome fear is by courageously confronting it, not to fight it or discount it. I am learning not to run away from it, but to make myself face it head on.

My little granddaughter likes to have me make shadow pictures on the wall with my hands. Huge, eerie animals take various shapes as the light reflects the shadows made by my hands.

When an unusually grotesque figure appears, she gives a squeal of terror. Facing her fear head-on, she says, "Don't, Grammy. I want to see the really thing — your hand." I put the light into direct focus and show her that only my hands are there. The shadowy figure of fear vanishes when she sees the reality.

Many times I have been haunted by the specter of fear. As I reach out into the light by faith, knowing that God is in charge, I am no longer afraid. Even the small and pesky fears scamper like shadows before the Son of God.

When we let fear absorb us, it produces a darkness in life. We become slaves to it, no longer free to live the life that God has planned for us — a life that is joyous and unafraid.

What about the tomorrows? At the present moment, our nation is in a moral and economic and political crisis. We are concerned for the future of our country and how we will be affected as individuals.

Many of us are concerned whether we can make

it financially through the economic crises of rising prices and shortages of the necessities of life. These are the pressures of circumstances and situations that will not disappear. They are there to be faced. This is the way of life.

Jesus recognized this and He knew that the human reaction is to be anxious and fearful. That is why He promises, "Don't be anxious about tomorrow. God will take care of your tomorrow too" (Matthew 6:34, TLB).

Anxiety can be destructive to the human body. It is said that the little ants pick a carcass cleaner than a lion. When we let little things worry us, we bring on ourselves an anxiety neurosis that will in time rob us of the best that life has to offer.

If we can have a childlike faith, we can believe that our Father cares about us. This assurance will be our stronghold. To really believe this is to discover that it is fabulously true.

Recently I visited an Alcoholics Anonymous meeting and listened with interest to the stories of several who had found victory over alcoholism. The same theme was there: "We live only twenty-four hours at a time. That is all that we can hope for."

The secret of their victories is the idea that Christ so wants all of us to grasp — that of living one day at a time, today.

Anxiety for the future is based on the unknown and becomes exaggerated in our minds. The result is an agony of spirit.

Since I am a woman living alone, the fear of the future often haunts me. What will happen to me in my old age? What if illness should overtake me so that I could no longer earn my living? These are questions that many of us ask. God gives us the positive answer. We are not alone.

I am not alone. No fear on earth can overcome the knowledge that there are two of us, God and myself, to meet every possible situation. This doesn't necessarily mean that these situations could not happen to me, as they do to many. What it does mean is that I have a source greater than my own strength and power on which I can draw. This makes the difference.

I have often asked myself, "Do I really trust God? Am I ready to go into the dangers of human existence with a calm and peace in my heart because I am really sure God will take care of me?"

There are times when I have reached this state of trust; fear and anxiety fade out. Then there are other times when I take these anxieties back into my own hands, and life takes on a somber tone. What I need to do is to stay in a position of trust, remembering that God is here and nothing can sustain me except Him.

One night, as I sat listening to the Philadelphia Symphony Orchestra, the drummer had a solo part. He started with a muffled beat of his drum. Then the sounds grew louder, still retaining a slow, measured rhythm. This left the listeners with a feeling of heaviness and sadness.

Later on in the symphonic number, the drummer again had the solo part. This time the master drummer changed the pitch of the drumhead and increased the beat to an allegro. The music was light and fast. It had the beat of a dance and the tonal picture was a rhythm of joy. Fear and anxiety give life a drumbeat of heaviness but Christ can change this into the beat of a dance of deliverance.

New life patterns evolve from the old and there is always the challenge that each day can be better than the day before.

CHAPTER NINE

The Yesterdays

Enjoy the blessings of the day if God sends them: and the evils bear patiently and sweetly; for this day only is ours. We are dead to yesterday, and not born to tomorrow.

— Jeremy Taylor

Setting out from small town surroundings to a new life in a city, we instinctively pause to look back at the old familiar scenes that we are leaving. We try to soak every item of it all into our memory. Then we turn and face out into the new and unknown larger world into which we are about to venture.

Frequently we return to the hometown for another look to recall its old and haunting memories. Although they are totally irrelevant to our present life, we continue to hold on to the memories of yesterday.

There is a three-day radius of time in which life seems to center — yesterday, today, tomorrow. Some of us become victims of our yesterdays and we discover our inability to cope with life in the today.

Life cannot be lived at its best if we cling to the failures and heartbreaks of yesterday, nor can we discover true happiness until we find release.

Periodically Joan seeks me out to report on her nights out on the town: drinking, drugs and sex. In one of her pensive moments, I asked her if she really found the happiness in life she seemed to be seeking so desperately.

"I don't know," she mused. "I believe there is only today to live life to the fullest. I sometimes wonder what real happiness might be like. There are times I do wish I could forget my yesterdays."

Her idea of living only in the today is right, even though her method of living it is not bringing her much happiness. What she has not discovered is a way of life that would bring release from her todays when they become the haunting yesterdays. The guilt is always there so that she is never really free to live a happy life in the now. We have talked much about this but as yet she has come to no decision.

It took me some time to grasp the truth that the past is over. Those things which had been sadly mishandled by me would not come again. When God entered my life, He walked through my yesterdays and brought healing to them. He set me free to invest in the today of life.

All of us at some time bring into the today of life some of our past. If we cling to these yesterdays for too long, we may lose the life that Christ had planned for us.

I have a friend whose home was broken by divorce. Heartbreak, loneliness, despair and disillusionment became an intimate part of her life as she continually relived her past experience.

Realizing she couldn't continue living on this level, she sought help from God. The situation had not changed; she was still divorced. But her attitude toward it changed. She moved from her hometown to another city and started a fresh life. With God's help and her willingness to release her past into His hands, her life took on a new tone and purpose.

In her job situation she found that there were many others who had been through the same heartbreaking experience and were searching for a meaning to life. She reached out in love and care for them. It was then that life became really meaningful for her. She now looks forward to each day with anticipation because she is learning to live one day at a time.

It is often difficult for us to realize that those yesterdays of ours, the hurts, the days of failure, are somehow involved in the now. As God works out His purpose in our lives from the yesterdays, there comes the time when we realize that we have accepted the words of Jesus who said, "Come to me, all of you who are tired from carrying your heavy loads, and I will give you rest" (Matthew 11:28, TEV), and we have found them to be true.

CHAPTER TEN

Loneliness

People are lonely because they build walls instead of bridges.

— *Joseph Fort Newton*

ANOTHER COMMON PROBLEM of our mutual humanity is loneliness. All of us have experienced human loneliness at some time or other. The loss of a loved one; an inability to make friends; divorce; despair, with no strength left to go on; children grown who have left home to live their own lives; various other situations all contribute to loneliness.

A friend who visited me in New York described her reaction to this strange city where she knew no one but me. As the people milled around her she said that she felt as though she were locked up in a world of thousands with only herself for company.

Being lonely hurts. It shatters a human heart. Allowed to continue, loneliness can consume a person to the point of withdrawal from an active participation in life.

Recently, in the *New York Post,* there was a report of the suicide of a young woman only twenty-nine years old. Life was just starting for her, yet it had already crushed her. She worked hard, prepared herself fully for her position and was making some progress in it. Yet it wasn't enough. She reached out to people only to find no response. No one seemed to love or care for her. Finding no answer to her loneliness, it made death her only hope.

Molly and Jim were a very close couple. Their lives centered in each other. Jim died suddenly. leaving Molly to face life alone. She tried everything to get over her loneliness. She sought release in gay parties, in the mad pursuit of buying things for herself, in never being alone. Yet the loneliness persisted. In talking with me one day she said she wished she could find someone who could love her as Jim had. I tried to help by sharing with her what God meant to me in my times of loneliness. As yet she has not discovered Him but has begun to express a yearning for someone greater than her loneliness.

There is the loneliness of a broken heart. So many have suffered the trauma of divorce and know the strange emptiness of returning to a house which had been filled with memories of happier yesterdays. Overwhelmed with a sense of failure and a fear for the future that must be faced alone, many seek release in alcoholism. Some, unable to bear the loneliness, become cases of despair in psychiatric records. Statistics report that suicide is three times greater among divorcees than among married women. If only they could know how much God loves and cares.

Loneliness is often one of my "hang-ups"; it can come to anyone who lives alone. Before I met Christ there were times it almost consumed me. My children were grown and had left home to live their own lives. This left an aching void which I used to try to fill by becoming immersed in my own interests, pleasures and sorrows. This loneliness grew because it stemmed from my selfishness and self-pity. I had marooned myself on my own little island.

I found that the key to overcoming loneliness is again stated in this fundamental principle laid down by Christ: "Love God with all your heart, your mind and being, and your neighbor as yourself."

One of the greatest things that God did for me was to break up my private life, making it a thoroughfare for others on the one hand and for Himself on the other. As I became involved with the needs of people, my own loneliness was dissipated. This gives me a continuous gift of a full life.

Dr. Erica Friedman, a noted psychiatrist, states: "Part of the answer to loneliness is having the courage to open your own door, reach out, knock on someone else's door and then ask if you can come in. Until a person learns how to go outside of himself, he will always be lonely."

CHAPTER ELEVEN

Love Versus Hate

He that cannot forgive others, breaks the bridge over which he himself must pass if he would ever reach heaven; for every one has need to be forgiven.

— *Edward Herbert*

ONE OF THE HEAVIEST BURDENS a person can carry is hatred. It seeps into a person so subtly that many times one is unaware of what is happening.

Hatred may have its source in anger towards another person and may be expressed in contempt. It is usually evoked by a clash of wills, a conflict of selfish interests, a struggle for power.

Anger, if it goes unchecked, can develop into a smoldering resentment. Self-pity, envy, a feeling of not being wanted or appreciated or loved can also grow into giant resentments. If we allow these to remain in us the wound festers and eats into the very fiber of our personalities.

Resentments unchecked can result in hatred toward another person. Hate is more injurious to the hater than to the hated. It destroys one's sense of values and objectivity. Not only does it do this, but in time it can bring on sickness that is physical.

Hatred makes one distrustful of others and shuts them out of a person's life. From distrust of others, there is a descent downward to loathing of oneself.

This can produce a stage of hopelessness from which there seems to be no way of escape.

The most difficult thing God asked of me was to forgive a person who had wronged me. I felt I had a right to my feeling of deep resentment which bordered on hatred. I clung tenaciously to this right.

As I continued to read and reread the Gospels, there came a growing conviction that God was making it mandatory that I forgive. His words, "For if you forgive other people their failures, your Heavenly Father will also forgive you. But if you will not forgive other people, neither will your Heavenly Father forgive you your failures" (Matthew 6:14, Phillips), haunted me. Then came the moment when I knew I must make a decision. Either I wanted to obey God and continue walking in this new way of life — or I didn't.

From previous experience I knew that this act of forgiveness could not be accomplished through my own doing. After a long struggle it was with a sense of relief that I gave my right to hold this resentment into God's hands. The resentment was replaced with the kind of love and caring that goes beyond the individual and sees his needs. This was God-given.

In God's love there is a strange transforming power and healing. To forgive the hurt inflicted by another takes more than a human can do on his own. The net result for the person who gives up his resentment is a sense of well-being, freedom and a joyous outlook on life.

Christ emphasizes the absolute necessity of a frank, free and unconditional forgiveness, no matter how deep the injuries or how often they are repeated. This forgiveness is not a once-for-all experience but a continual surrender of one's rights to resent people as new situations arise. This is not easy. God further asks of us, as Christians, that we always take the first step toward reconciliation. Our reward is a sense of inner peace and love that helps us to sleep well at night and to live well by day.

From various experiences I have come to the conclusion that this new way of life is not an easy one. It is a demanding and challenging way. All that is noble in us has to be hammered into us by the hard things which need elimination and against which we often angrily protest.

CHAPTER TWELVE

After Death?

We picture death as coming to destroy; let us rather picture Christ as coming to save. We think of death as ending; let us rather think of life as beginning, and that more abundantly. We think of losing; let us think of gaining. . . . We think of parting; let us think of meeting. We think of going away; let us think of arriving. And as the voice of death whispers "You must go from earth," let us hear the voice of Christ saying, "You are but coming to Me!"

— *N. Macleod*

My previous philosophy had assured me that what there was of life was entirely in the now. Life should be lived in its fullness. Death was the end of one's dreams, one's ambitions, one's life.

With the acceptance of this new life from God, there came a glimmer of hope — the possibility of a life after death. Belief in this life after death doesn't come in a moment's time. It comes as we walk with God, loving Him, obeying Him and trusting Him.

Most of us find it difficult to break away from the common way of judging reality through the experiences of the five senses. We can believe easily in the things we can see and touch. That is why it becomes difficult to believe in a life after death. There is no tangible evidence of survival.

As our faith grows in God, we come to realize God didn't create humans to end after a few fleeting years on earth. He went to too much trouble making sure we could return to Him in this life not to have us continue on into the adventure of the eternal. Death is not the end. Christ promised us life after death. Jesus' words have great meaning for me: "I am the one who raises the dead and gives them life again. Anyone who believes in me, even though he dies like anyone else, shall live again. He is given eternal life for believing in me and shall never perish" (John 11:25, 26, TLB).

Having found Him worthy of my trust in tangible experience, I can trust Him with the unknown.

There is loneliness in death. Many times a person in crisis cannot be reached by words. With a dying patient in particular, there is that horrible, distressing loneliness at the end. Words won't bring comfort for they cannot be heard. The human touch is the only thing that can tell him he is not so alone.

There is truth in the statement: "Every man must bear his own pain. Every man must endure his own sorrow. Every man must face his own death alone." No other person can do any of these things for us. Each one of us has to come to grips with these significant things in life. Having faced them, there is deep meaning in God's promise that He will never leave us alone in any situation.

Death was a very fearful thing for me. I loved life and the thought of it ending was hard to accept. But as I continued in the God-relationship, I felt less afraid. Christ is alive and to His followers He promises that because He lives they shall live also.

We know little about the beyond because no one has returned to tell us about it. But Christ is there and that is all that matters. He has promised that we will live again. There were times when I believed and there were times I had doubts.

One day, while walking along a country road in the early spring, I sat down on a rock to rest. Three days had passed since I had stood by my sister's coffin. I felt a loneliness at the loss.

Again the question kept flowing through my mind, "Is there life after death?" I bowed my head, asking God to give me some sort of reassurance that there is a life beyond.

Without thinking what I was doing, I pulled a spear of grass. As I looked at it, God showed me that life does indeed go on. Nature demonstrates the fact that no matter in the universe is ever really annihilated. Each springtime new life emerges from death. A God who can do this can bring life to us after death, this I have come to believe. God reveals this truth to others in different ways, but He used this method to reassure me.

Most important is the joy of the Easter message. The grave could not hold Christ and because He lives, we too shall live. He has promised us life eternal. Our part is to love and follow Him.

There is the certainty that death for each one of us is just one heartbeat from eternity. What we do with our lives here can make such a difference.

Martin and Shirley are friends of mine. We started this new life with Christ about the same time. They had been attending a conference and Martin had participated in the program. He had just finished speaking when he slumped to the floor. His death was instantaneous. It was a great shock to his wife and three children. I received a letter from Shirley who wrote the following:

We all have our tears, of course, and as Steve said last night, "It's not so much fun coming home now from college" and I know what he means. . . . Marty grew closer and closer to God this past year. I believe our love for each other in the natural sense was transcended by our love in the spirit toward the Lord. When sadness comes, it seems God sweeps it away and there is a deep peace and joy in our hearts. I can say with all my heart, God has given us a taste of the Resurrection and some day in the future we will join Marty in that eternal world. Of this I am sure.

Since I knew this couple for years, Shirley's testimony of faith has strengthened my own faith in a life after death. It is a trust given by God who came to show us that His way gives life eternal. The key to it all is faith, and faith stems from a love and trust in God.

I belong to God — not only for the few years on this earth — but for eternity. Because He lives, I too shall live.

CHAPTER THIRTEEN

Fulfilled Life

Happiness is neither within us only, or without us; it is the union of ourselves with God.

— *Blaise Pascal*

THE MOST DESIRABLE THINGS in life are hope, peace, joy and happiness. People will go to any extent in their search for these qualities.

Jesus, the Teacher of truth, said that if we followed His way, we would practice happiness and have a full life. It is as simple as that, yet we continue our search.

Happiness and joy are twin qualities. All of us strive to find happiness. This state of contentment does not come easily. Pleasure is frantically pursued in the hope that happiness can be found in its offerings. The result is satisfaction for the moment but it never seems to be lasting. The frantic search ever continues.

Along with others of my acquaintance, I pursued a good position in the business world. That is not wrong in itself, but in making it "god," there was no lasting happiness. We were never satisfied and personally I was always left with a feeling of emptiness.

Money in itself doesn't seem to be the answer.

We pick up the daily papers and read of suicides among those who are blessed with this world's goods.

Happiness and joy are God's gifts to us. He came to set at liberty those oppressed. He brought good news to the poor. When Jesus passed through the towns while here on earth, sorrows were healed. He restored people to health, strength, and cleanness. It is a joy to be set free from something.

Christ brings a richness to life that leaves a person filled with a sense of well-being. Life becomes crowded with interests. The key that opens this life to us is the giving of self to the only One who can release us so that it becomes possible to move into a satisfying existence. The exciting thing is that many people are working at it and succeeding.

True happiness is found in continuous communion with God, putting all trust in Him, and in the unselfish spending of life for others. This kindly, unselfish way of using life is the characteristic of the Christian who has been liberated by God.

Love is the key to joy and happiness. Joy is urged upon us only for the purpose of teaching us how to be alive. When we are in harmony with God there is joy. However, we have to practice this attitude.

Often I have started the day with a despairing outlook, wondering if any good can come of it. Then comes the moment when I realize that God is my Father and I am His child. Because of this, I can be filled with a joy that comes from deep within my soul and there is a change from despair to happiness in my outlook.

Many times joy comes out of pain and suffering.

Some of our days will be dark and dreary but there will be glorious experiences and happy moments. Sometimes joy comes silently to us through a time of sadness when we look into a face of someone who understands. This is a depth of joy that is given to us and which brings a benediction to our lives.

Christianity is not superficial. It recognizes pain, sin, injustice and degradation of varying sorts existing in today's world. Yet Christ dares to declare that in spite of all these imperfections, we can find a life of joy and happiness.

Our world is in great turmoil. There are wars, murders, food shortages, job shortages, and we wonder how it is possible to stay in an attitude of peace. Peace of mind is a gift from God. This spirit of tranquillity develops from within a person and starts with a trust in God that no matter what happens, God is there. When the storms of life beat against us again and again, Jesus Christ gives this assurance to us, "My peace I give unto you: not as the world giveth, give I unto you . . ." (John 14:27).

Trusting God wholeheartedly, laying my whole being at His disposal, holding back nothing — it is then that a peace that passes understanding can be mine. When I take back into my own hands the life I had given to Him and try running it my own way, I lose the peace I so want.

Peace comes from a mind clean of a sense of guilt. The moment I have done an evil thing, it lingers with me. The nasty remark that I made to another and tried to put from my mind, hoping time would wash it away, robs me of this peace. Until I admit this wrong to God and seek forgiveness and then ask forgiveness of the one I wronged, I will have no peace. My peace hinges on a loving relationship with God and with my fellowman.

To find peace of mind does not mean an escape into a dream world but more effective participation in a real world. In the heart of the tornado is the eye which is the center of calm.

When I crossed the Atlantic to visit my daughter, the ship on which I was crossing rode into a heavy storm. The water piled high over the ship at times. One of the ship's officers passed by our table and stopped to remark about the severity of the storm. He said it was too bad we couldn't drop the ship down to great depths because that was where the calm waters were.

There are times it seems as though the storms of life would sink us, but we can draw into the depths of our souls and find a calm placed there by God from which we can draw strength. This power of Jesus Christ can heal our tension and stress.

One of God's gifts to us is hope in ourselves, for the present and the future. We are living in times when it seems almost impossible to hope that there will be a change for the better. Yet we are urged to continue hoping. When a person loses hope he is doomed to die.

So many of the younger generation have become disillusioned with the world and are losing hope. This despair drives them into all sorts of things, including drugs and alcohol, hoping to find release — but never really finding it.

As we lose the vision of what life can become, we lose hope, and life holds no future or joy. Outside of love, which is God's greatest gift, hope is His second gift to us. This attitude of hope is dependent upon our love for God and the knowledge that His love for us is constant. It is then that we can know the fullness of life with God's basic gifts to us: peace, happiness, joy, hope, and love.

CHAPTER FOURTEEN

Journey Inward

Nothing will make us so charitable and tender to the faults of others, as, by self-examination, thoroughly to know our own.

— *Francis Fenelon*

Nobody knows more about human nature in all of its complexities and intricacies than Jesus Christ. When I was confronted with the command of Christ that I love my neighbor as myself, I was intrigued with the idea. How could this come about?

Each one of us has within himself a personal dualism. There is the self that people see and the real self which is kept very carefully hidden. This enables us to go through life playing a variety of roles. At times it makes us wonder who we really are. If this dualism continues, how can it be possible to love another as oneself?

Life begins for the person who meets himself for the first time. If we let God wipe the dust from our eyes we will be able to see ourselves as we really are in comparison to Him. Often the reflection is grotesque and we are shocked at the image. This revelation of the inner self shows our cover-ups, our role-playing abilities, as well as our self-centered lives. This dual self we thought so great needs a change.

A life united with the life of God is no longer a

dualism. The moment we say "I will" to Him, the dualism will cease. God brings a oneness into our lives. This is accomplished through an open and honest relationship with the self and God, with the self and self, and with the self and others. The turning point comes when we surrender the ego center to God and it becomes His center.

The ego-centered person is a person who is out of tune with God and finds it impossible to love someone else. This makes the relationship between two people lack reality. God removes the camouflage from this ego, enabling us to have a greater purpose than before, as well as making it possible to have an in-depth relationship with another person.

A proper self-love often begins when we find that others love and accept us despite our failures. This relationship is found between Christians which enables each to grow in love. We can never love others or experience a proper self-love unless we have had the experience of being loved.

This dual personality which we possess cannot be brought into a unity through our own accomplishments and Christ doesn't ask impossibilities of us. His supreme offer is the power of our re-creation which enables a new self to emerge. This is the self that can truly love another "as oneself."

To love self and to take care of the needs of the self is an ever-present human urge. To love another with the same degree of love is divine. To do this, God must touch the self-life in order to bring it out of its self-orbit into that greater orbit — the love for others.

114

Jesus was aware of the importance of a comparative love which was to be the guideline for loving one's neighbor. This goes beyond loving only the people we like.

What Christ might really be asking, in everyday language, is, "Do you really want your enemy to have the good things of life, or do you want to see him crushed for the things he has done to you?" This is a real challenge, since the philosophy of the times is that our enemy should get what is coming to him. Many secretly delight in seeing this happen.

Self-abasement is a disgrace to God who created us with all our potentials. When I became a Christian I was afraid that He might ask that I become a "nothing," giving up everything. Not so. To each of us He has given a uniqueness and certain abilities. True love is having a deep, joyous respect for this self. What God asks of us is that we always be mindful that any ability, capability or potential is His gift to us to be used for His glory.

Jesus doesn't want to pour us into molds. He made us to be individuals who dare to dream, to long to be more than we are, to love more. What God wants is to be the source — the recognized source.

If there is any field of life in which we must have the utmost integrity, it is in the realm of our religious life. This same integrity is a part of our relationship with one's self and with others. This "realness" must invade our innermost being, for God hates sham and make-believe.

When we become Christians, it is important that we be very realistic about ourselves. Even though

Christ has healed the dualism, we are not perfect and can only aim for perfection. Only God is perfect. The acceptance of our own imperfections will help us to be more understanding in regard to the imperfections of our neighbors.

Because God has accepted us and loves us as we are, we in turn are freed to love our neighbor as ourselves. We can only get our own sense of worth from knowing that we are precious in God's sight.

When I was studying to become a concert pianist, my teacher — a master artist — would often play the music along with me on another piano. This would happen only when the passage of music was especially difficult.

First he would show me how it should be played. Then he would say, "Now let's do it together." We would go over and over again the most difficult phrases, using the right touch and tempo until I had mastered them. They were no longer just black blobs on lines. Through the help of the master they began to form a picture of tonal beauty which became pleasing both to him and to the listener.

This is what the Master of life does with anyone who is willing to give the self-life over to Him for training.

CHAPTER FIFTEEN

Our Mutual Humanity

Love never reasons, but profusely gives; gives,
like a thoughtless prodigal, its all, and trembles
then lest it has done too little.

— *Hannah More*

In order to love others as ourselves, we need to start with some basics. We are human beings, a conglomerate of good and bad instincts. As we recognize our own weaknesses, we are able to accept the weaknesses as well as the strengths of others. We have the same needs. We want to feel that this life is worthwhile. We are dependent on one another for our physical needs in order to survive. Most of all we want to be loved and appreciated by others.

Jesus was the supreme example of a life given completely to God first and then to others. His days on earth were filled: touching the sick with healing, listening to others, caring and helping them. Jesus was not a dreamer. He was a doer amid very real relationships. He offered friendship to the friendless. He loved those who were considered the dregs of society. His life tells us that if we pass through this needy world and remain self-absorbed and show no sympathy to the needs of other people then our religion is a self-deception and a sham.

One of the greatest things that God does for us as

Christians is to break up our private lives to become channels through which flows God's love for others. Love has to have hands to do things, feet to carry and hearts to feel. Our service to others won't be given just in emergencies but in the daily doing of the extra touch in the little things of life. This is what God intends to do through us.

I was one of many in our community involved in various social actions which included giving donations to the poor, money for various fund-raising drives, fighting for the rights of the minority, etc. All this was good. But I could bring no hope to the person as an individual.

Upon deciding to take seriously the claims of Christ on my life, things began to happen. First there was an involvement with people. Up to then I picked people I liked for friends and the rest could go along their own way. Now I could enfold them in my love as I had become enfolded within the great love of God. I could go a step beyond the doing and become acquainted with some of the people involved on the receiving end of our social action.

I once heard a story that illustrates the difference. There was a father who told the story of the three bears every night to his children. It was their favorite story and they requested it over and over again. Dad became weary of the same old story and tried to think of some way to get out of it. He thought to himself, "Why not have it recorded and played for them? This way they will hear my voice and it will be the same story." He did this.

Then he sat and read his paper in peace. But after

listening to the recording, one little boy came downstairs and climbed into his father's lap. The rest of the children climbed up after him.

The father, surprised, said, "Son, didn't you hear the story and wasn't it my voice?"

"Yes," the little boy replied, "but it doesn't put its arms around my neck." A philosophy of social action alone gives only to the physical needs of the person, leaving him with the same despair and hopelessness that he had before.

As we walk in this way of Christ, we find that it involves our time, our interest, our caring, our finances, and most of all our love. This way of life is daring, adventurous and positive.

At the same time there is a risk involved. This is the most difficult aspect of love. We must risk being misunderstood at times.

There are times when, because of some relationship where we have been rejected, it is painful to love. We often retreat from any close relationship in which warmth or love may prove a threat because of our fear of being hurt. God asks us to risk ourselves and our hurts in loving others for His sake.

This new life given by God is not restricted to the religious society but encompasses the secular world. There is no separation, for God's way is a complete involvement with all of life. The "love your neighbor as yourself" relationship encompasses the home, the job, the church, the community and the world. Putting into action this principle of love in each area can change people and circumstances. Love is an activating force.

Someone has said that all of life is contained in the opening of one door; then, in a brief moment, another door opens and we pass into eternity. When this last door is opened, it will not be what we have accomplished for self that will count, but what we have given of this self to God and to others.

CHAPTER SIXTEEN

It Starts in the Home

Strength of character may be acquired at work, but beauty of character is learned at home. There the affections are trained. There the gentle life reaches us, the true heaven life. In one word, the family circle is the supreme conductor of Christianity.

— *Henry Drummond*

THE FIRST PLACE to begin living this new way of life is in the home and this is usually the most difficult spot. It is here that relationships are most intimate and most taken for granted. Also it is here, because of this intimacy, that the pressures are greatest. Why are we unkind to the persons we love the most? The sharp words, the insults, the degrading of one another cut deep into our souls. There results a rift in the intimate relationship which, if not resolved, can result in a drifting apart.

Jesus says that it is the little foxes that spoil the vines and it seems to be the little things that upset the tranquillity of the home. We are irked if the meal isn't on time, or if Billy forgot to pick up the paper, or for any number of small things. Tempers clash over the smallest of incidents, setting the whole house in an uproar. We are not perfect and we would not be human if we didn't become angry at times. This is life. What Jesus asks of us is the humbling experience of admitting our imperfections and asking forgiveness. In such sharing come release and healing.

One factor that seems to be contributing to the problems of the new generation is the breakdown of family life. Home is the center and stabilizing force in the growth of a child. There is an innate desire to belong and a need for each other. That is why it is so devastating when family ties are broken.

It is in the home that the child learns to meet life's problems in everyday confrontation with the other members of the family. This is the place where he starts to learn to love and care for others, which prepares him for his place in the greater society. We, as Christians, can bring love into our home relationships which will stabilize our homes and make them centers where our children can find themselves.

Much of my time was spent earning our livelihood and I was absorbed in seeing that my children were properly dressed, well fed, had the right relationships with people and did the right things. I was so busy with all of this that I lost the art of listening. I love my daughters deeply. Yet, in the give and take of everyday living, I realized that very often I allowed the best of life to slip by. Part of this new life in Christ is learning to be a "good listener." So many times we get caught up in the myriad of things that have to be done that we are just "surface" listeners rather than "depth" listeners. Consequently, we don't hear what our children are trying to say to us. Because my job took me away from the home eight hours each day, I found that I had to work harder to keep the communication lines open with my daughters.

In today's world, it is not easy to keep a loving

relationship going between parent and child with communication lines open. The new morality, the drug scene, the countless other things that must be faced in our society often bring friction in the home as the parent tries to save the child from them. The final celebration of a graduation was to be an all-night beach party. One young woman wanted desperately to go because she wanted to be part of the crowd. Her parents gave a flat "no" to the idea. This created a hostility between them.

The parents could only think of the dire things that might happen at an all-night beach party. But to the daughter it meant losing face, being a square, and facing the ridicule of her friends. A deep bitterness sprang up between them. Not knowing what to do, the mother decided to apply the principle of love to the situation and see if it would work. She asked her daughter to talk over this situation with her. In sharing openly and honestly together what they both felt about the idea, they could hear each other for the first time. The circumstances didn't change but the relationship did improve a little and they were able once again to communicate.

One thing I had to learn in this new way of life was to release my daughters into God's hands and not to try to run their lives for them. We mothers are so sure we have the answers to everything and that we know what is best. After all, haven't we lived longer and learned a few lessons which we would like to pass on to our children? True! But as they approach adulthood we must release the reins with only a gentle touch now and then. If I am to love my girls

127

"as myself" — as God commanded — then they must be free to walk through life in their own way and to learn its lessons through their own experiences. My part is to hold them in prayer and let God take care of them.

Because we feel we know best what is right for our children, we often try to pour them into our molds of living, wanting them to choose a career to our liking and for which we feel that they are best fitted. God had to show me that each life must be lived according to His plan, not mine. It wasn't until I could release these girls of mine into His care that we could all be free to be ourselves. Love becomes more than a word — it becomes action.

A friend of mine had an intelligent and beautiful girl for a daughter. As in some families, there was a generation gap and this girl was estranged from her father. The mother was deeply concerned over the situation and had spoken about it often.

Several of us, including this mother and daughter, planned a day together with our families for a picnic and fun. As we sat around talking, one of the other girls asked this daughter how her father was. With bitterness, she blurted out, "I don't know and I don't care. I hate him."

As we talked with her about this, she finally admitted that she was very unhappy and miserable.

I took her to one side, when the others wandered off, and shared with her that I had once known resentment that deeply. I told her how I had started praying about the situation and about the gradual change that took place when I surrendered this re-

128

sentment to God. I dared her to try praying this simple paryer each day and see what would happen: "God, bless my father."

Her reply at the moment was, "I couldn't."

At a later time she decided to try this experiment just to see what might happen. She was so miserable that she was ready to try anything and felt that she had nothing to lose.

One day, as her father stood with his back to the fire, she said she obeyed an impulse to run and throw her arms around him. Later she wrote me, "I've found my father again and I am so happy and so is he." A human love which had lain buried in hatred for several years was brought to life by a divine love, and through prayer a home relationship was changed.

Christ affects every relationship and brings into these areas the healing so desperately needed if we seek His help.

CHAPTER SEVENTEEN

God in the Office

A new step in the sanctification of secular life is needed for the rejuvenation of the world. Not only will the spirit of Christ overflow into secular life . . . as well as among monks dedicated to the search for perfection; but a kind of divine simplification will help people to realize that the perfection of human life does not consist in a stoic athleticism of virtue or in a humanly calculated application of holy recipes, but rather in a ceaselessly increasing love, despite our mistakes and weaknesses, between the Uncreated Self and the Created Self.

— *Jacques Maritain*

It DIDN'T TAKE TOO LONG to discover that one of the most challenging areas in which I could put the love of God into practice would be the business world. It is in this field that selfish ambition so often becomes our prime motivation and we are apt to disregard the methods we use to reach our goal.

I have always liked my work and I, too, have always wanted to be successful. There is nothing wrong in the desire to do one's best to succeed. But when my march to success requires trampling upon another to reach it, it is all wrong. I used to feel that the only way to the top was to be selfish, pushy, concentrating utterly on winning what I had set out to attain.

But Christ is showing me that it is possible to have these solid and substantial things while still giving my life for others, not caring what happens as long as God is in control. My true success must be rooted in my fellow worker. If I am to love this person as myself, which Christ requests of me, then his well-being becomes an imperative of my life.

This, many times, is very difficult since it involves my own future.

At one time or another, we have all encountered injustices in our work life. It is so easy to lash out in bitterness, and so difficult to accept these injustices. It is even harder to love those who have committed the injustices against us. There is a narrow margin between becoming a doormat and letting love be the ruling factor in these situations. How we apply the sensitivity of Christ to these happenings will be the basis on which we learn to "love our neighbor as ourselves," and still maintain our own integrity and identity.

I found that this new way of living affected my attitude towards the work itself. There are parts of every job that are disagreeable and I find it very easy to put these parts aside until some future time. I am sorry to say the "future time" had a way of making this task always the last thing on the list. If I am to be open and honest in all things, I find I must give of my best to whatever I do, and this includes my work life.

One of the first things God challenged me with in my everyday business relationships was to face up to any wrong attitude towards another. As an executive of the company, I was involved with all the employees. It is so easy to like those who produced on the job, who were outgoing and friendly. It was very difficult to like those who gave one a "hard time." My thought, at first, was that as long as I could be patient with the unlikable by ignoring them, that was all God would require of me.

I soon found this was not so. One morning as I passed by the desk of one of the girls, she touched my arm and said softly, "I must talk with you. I know that you don't like me, but I must talk with someone and you are my boss." It was true, I didn't like her. She was one of the to-be-ignored workers. She had caused no end of trouble to her co-workers and the only reason she was still employed was due to her business skills.

As she spoke to me, there came the realization that Christ asked more of me than just mere patience with another. He was challenging me to become involved with the hurts of someone I did not like.

I asked her to come with me to my office and I closed the door. I motioned to her to sit down. She then burst into tears, pouring out her troubles both with her business associates and her problems at home. I asked God to help me to love her and be of some assistance to her. I felt the best possible approach was an honest and open sharing of how I had felt about her and how God was now to bring about a new relationship in our business life together. This encounter not only changed her own outlook on life, but I found new avenues of bringing God's love to bear in other business relationships that were sometimes difficult. Many times this experiment has been very trying, but love does change relationships and, thereby, situations.

Behind the facade of the beligerent individual I have found a person with hidden needs: perhaps full of fear, perhaps needing someone just to care, perhaps lonely and with no one to listen. There is no separation of the religious life from the secular life. God wants to be in all of life, and His presence does make a great difference.

A few days after discovering Christ to be real in my life, I was attending a cocktail party prior to a business dinner meeting. Six of us were sitting around the table together discussing various problems. Joan musingly remarked, "Life is such a monotonous thing. You wake up — eat — go to work — party — go to bed, and that is it. The next day it is the same routine. You are born and then you die. There seems to be no meaning to life and there is such an emptiness. Dear God, I wish something would fill the void."

With some diffidence I said, "God can fill the void." Joan looked at me as though I had taken leave of my senses. They all stared at me and one of the others remarked, "What brought that on?" I responded, "If you really want to hear about it, I will tell you."

For lack of anything better to talk about, they urged me to continue. I shared with them the emptiness of my own life, my purposelessness, until the night I had found God. I told them of the difference He had made in my life in a very short time and that the emptiness had completely gone. Life had taken on new meaning and had become exciting and worthwhile. They threw questions at me until it was time for the meeting. As we were entering the dining room, Ruth asked me to meet her for dinner the next evening, as she wanted to pursue the subject further. I agreed to meet her at the restaurant.

The next night over dinner we talked earnestly about God and the difference He can make in life. Like myself, Ruth was a career woman. She had been in the business world for twenty years and was vice-president of a large banking system. Yet she, too, experienced the same feeling of emptiness I had felt.

After talking for some time, Ruth finally said she would like to try this new way of life. There seemed to be nothing to lose and much to be gained. That night she made her decision.

The next day I had a call from Ruth and she confirmed her commitment of the previous night, adding that she felt as though she had come alive for the first time in her life. She, too, knew that God was real for she had met Him. As she was leaving in a couple of days for a world tour, I wished her a marvelous time and told her to drop me a line if she had a chance.

On the morning she was to leave, she was stricken with a heart attack and died within two hours. How glad I was she had found the love and peace of God before her adventure into the eternal.

Through sharing the discovery of this new life, God has become increasingly real in my own life.

CHAPTER EIGHTEEN

Why Church?

An every-day religion — one that loves the duties of our common walk; one that makes an honest man; one that accomplishes an intellectual and moral growth in the subject; one that works in all weather, and improves all opportunities, will best and most healthily promote the growth of a church and the power of the Gospel.

—Horace Bushnell

Until now church had little meaning for me. As an outside observer I felt many of the churches held Christianity as a theory to be accepted rather than a life to be daily and actively lived out. Then there were other churches so involved with social reforms and social action programs that there was little time left for the healing process of the inner man's soul.

As I had already spent much time in the past, in the name of the Church, raising funds for various charities, prison work, integration and other humane activities, I couldn't see why a return to the Church was necessary.

I wanted to be more than a traditionalist, merely conforming to church rules. Could I find the answer in the Church? There was an inner insistence that I become an active participant in some church.

In reading the Book of Acts, I was thrilled with the account of the early church. In spite of its imperfections, it set in motion the mighty force of the love of the resurrected Christ. Its impact on the world has been made through the ages. There seemed to be power generated in worshiping and working together. Along with many others I felt, that in some instances, today's church had lost the vision that justifies its existence. Therefore it was difficult to return to active participation in an institution I had held aloof from for some time.

In my search for a church home, I found the churches that were really making an impact on the community were those in which members were being led into a real, vital, honest relationship with God through Jesus Christ. God's Church has no denominational barriers. Such churches are taking their places in the community by serving God in every possible way, but always through His love and strength. We hear constantly that the Church must be relevant. But to what? The Christian religion is first an interrelationship between man and God. It then becomes interrelated and interlocked with human living.

There are countless numbers of people looking for a meaning to life and not finding it. Today's person wants to find a resource to help when death comes, jobs are lost, people disappoint, health wanes, and the future holds nothing but darkness.

It is true that the Church doesn't exist for the purpose of answering all questions or clearing up all the mysteries of life. Its purpose of existence should be to show mankind that a new life is possible if we can trust the Lord Jesus Christ. What we seek to discover is how we can find strength in the resources of God to overcome the circumstances of life that try to crush us. Christianity has little meaning to the man in the street if it does not show him that Christ is the Son of the living God who meets his needs.

My approach to church started with a small group of ten women who met once or twice a month in one another's homes. We had spent some time delving into the various religions of the world, seeking to find what each had to offer. A week or so after I had started walking in this new way of life, I shared with this group what had happened to me and gave them each a copy of the book that had brought me into this new life-style. One by one we came to know the living Christ in a very real way. We started to share this new life with others in our families and in the church.

The outreach was not confined to the immediate church which we attended. Wherever we were, we found that people basically have the same problems and needs we ourselves have. In sharing our problems and needs in prayer, and in caring for one another, we began to have a fellowship in depth. In this openness, honesty, and caring relationship, we had the freedom to admit that none of us had it made. We didn't need to pretend perfection for we had not "arrived," but were only pilgrims on a journey.

Our service to the community had a more personal touch because we were able to see people as persons who had real needs. These needs extended beyond the physical necessities we had tried to meet previously. We shared with them the joy of becoming acquainted with the source of their needs whose power can transform the inner person endowing it with great strengths to face any trying circumstances.

The church became more meaningful to me as my attitude towards it began to change. It became evident that there is power in worshiping God and working together for Him. Also I discovered that if I bring nothing of myself into the church life, I will find nothing in its confines.

In our newfound zeal within the organized church, some of us frequently tended to try to pour others into our molds. We looked for the sameness of religious experience, forgetting that our God is an innovator.

Neither is God one who can be poured into a mold and marked "this is God." He is elusive in nature and cannot be pinpointed in any one conception of Him. All nature reflects this diversity for there is no monotony in His creation. We discovered that the Christian experience need not be monotonous either. Each person has a unique relationship with God which is his or her very own and for which each is responsible.

Just recently, I experienced a new meaning to corporate prayer as we bowed together as a congregation while the pastor offered to God our needs, the needs of our country and the needs of the world. The words of Jesus, "Where two or three are gathered together in my name, there am I in the midst . . ." (Matthew 18:20) became reality and I felt the need of corporate worship in the church.

Regardless of the faults of the Church, and there are many, there is strength in unity. This might be one reason why Christ called the Church into being, that together with Him we might stand against the evil powers in the world. We, as Christians, are the channel of His love to all humanity.

Unless, within the church structure, we can put into practice the principles Jesus so carefully taught, there is little chance that we will do this in the world around us. It is so easy to criticize a person who fails, forgetting that in reality we are all human beings prone to error.

The honeybee does not benefit from the honey it gathers each day. It lives and survives from the honey gathered by the bees who lived before it. You might say it profits from the "collective" experiences of bees which previously gathered the honey that sustains the present bee colony. Isn't this like the member of the Church universal? The experiences of those of ages past have brought him the joy and the need of God's Church for his survival.

I know that God will triumph and the Church will still be able to extend this very real invitation:

"We want you to be with us in this — in this fellowship with the Father, and Jesus Christ his Son. We must write and tell you about it, because the more that fellowship extends, the greater the joy it brings to us who are already in it."

I John 1:3,4 (Phillips)

145

CHAPTER NINETEEN

This Is My World Too!

If the tender, profound and sympathizing love, practiced and recommended by Jesus, were paramount in every heart, the loftiest and most glorious ideas of human society would be realized and little be wanting to make this world a kingdom of heaven.

— *F. W. Krummacher*

A TRULY FULL AND HAPPY CHRISTIAN LIFE is involvement with the needs of our world. Our own country has the most affluent society in the world but this apparently has not added much happiness or significance to life. Basking in our own comforts, we tend to shrink from the upsets and dangers of open discipleship. Yet, through the power that Christ gives to us, we can be master over anything that can happen to us and we can indeed bring change into this world of ours.

The Christian often says, "But I am only one. What can I contribute to make the world a better place in which to live?" Many Christians have the philosophy that this world is not our home. Therefore they need not become involved in it to any degree. But Jesus was actively involved with the conditions of this world even though He knew He was only going to be here such a short time. He has said to us, in so many ways, that we are to occupy and keep busy until He comes. This is a part of living the Christian life.

Our political situations in this country have left much to be desired. God can use us by our involvement in community elections. I have a friend who ran for mayor in one of our larger cities and won the election. He was able to bring to the community an important impact for right by cleaning up some of the corruption existing in the area.

The problem of racial unrest is great in our country as well as in others. Yet each one of us can make a contribution toward bringing about change in this area by beginning in the home. We can teach our children that it is more important to love than to hate. We can assume responsibility for loving and helping those in our own everyday relationships who have so long been hated and hurt.

One Sunday morning I sat in church with a family whose son had become a drug addict. The parents were heartbroken. The mother was hoping that in the church they might find some strength to cope with the situation. The father had an air of hopelessness about him. We can stand with these parents in love as they go through the deep waters and try to find ways to help them.

I am concerned with the younger generation who are disenchanted with our society to the point of rioting, drunkenness and drug addiction. As I walk along the streets of New York and see these youths revolting against the current mode of thought and the traditions of the past, yet bringing into it no positive reforms, I wonder what caused this spirit of rebellion. I wonder what terrible emptiness is causing them to seek release in drugs and a nomadic life.

I am concerned with the dehumanization of man. Recently I read an article in one of the New York newspapers describing an attempted suicide by a young man waiting to jump from a high-story building. Crowds gathered below and some began chanting, "Jump, jump, jump." Until we realize the worth of another human being and begin to care again, we have lost the real essence of life. Some have forgotten that human relationships are a source of happiness and that all of life is made up of values and relationships. Jesus challenges us to involvement, even though it may be costly. He dares us to experiment with Him in bringing love and concern to bear upon the situations of life as we find them in this world of ours.

A social worker who was a friend of mine asked me to make a call on a woman who lived in the ghetto area while she was away on vacation. The afternoon I picked was steaming hot. Walking along the streets, I saw the garbage piled high and rats scampering in and out of the refuse.

Crossing the street, I found the house. Her apartment was a fourth-floor walk-up. I started the climb through the dirty halls and stairways that were falling apart from lack of upkeep. Reaching the top, I hammered on the chipped painted door. It opened, revealing a tiny white-haired woman. She invited me to come in and asked me to sit down in one of the two chairs in the room. The room was tiny with a small two-burner tabletop gas stove on which she prepared her meals. A dim bulb on the end of an electric cord swayed gently in the small breeze from

151

the open window and cast eerie shadows around the room. It was stifling hot in the room but the little old woman didn't seem to mind.

At first I was at a loss for conversation but soon the ice was broken and she talked freely. She was once a schoolteacher, now long retired and trying to stay alive on a small social security check. With the high cost of living she was finding it hard to get by. She had to stay in much of the time, as the climb up and down four flights was too much to take on daily. She didn't complain, but was just stating the facts of her life as they were.

She shared with me her faith in God and, as I listened, I marveled at the apparent acceptance of life as it is for her. Then she went on to tell about her neighbors' needs and wished that something could be done about finding clean, livable places for them to live.

As I got up to leave, I promised to call again. She was very lonely, as are so many of our aged citizens in a large city.

The ecological problems, the problem of crime, the drug problem, poverty — all seem to stem from one basic problem—man himself. Until God changes the heart of man, society will not change too much.

As Christians we know that these problems are our problems and that God asks our participation with Him in bringing some help to bear on them.

CHAPTER TWENTY

The Stranger—My Neighbor

The cure for all the ills and wrongs, the cares, the sorrows, and the crimes of humanity, all lie in that one word "love." It is the divine vitality that everywhere produces and restores life. To each and every one of us, it gives the power of working miracles if we will.

— *Lydia M. Child*

It is so easy to place people into categories. I had categorized people in little boxes, sealed and labeled: the hippies, the flower people, revolutionaries, alcoholics, prostitutes, the good people, the bad people, and so on. They were all seeking some purpose in life, doing their own thing. Yet these are the people whom God loves and asks us to love just as we love ourselves. We meet them on the bus, on the street, at the party, in the restaurant and in many public places. Outside my own intimate circle of acquaintances, individuals had long been faceless strangers to me. Now God began facing me with all sorts of people and demanding my involvement whether I chose it or not. As I become involved, I am continually learning the true meaning of love.

Love may mean just listening to another as he cries out his hurt. One evening, while coming home in a taxi, the driver blurted out, "Lady, would you mind if I just talk to you and you just listen?" This request wasn't unusual, for many cab drivers like to talk. I told him to go ahead.

His fiancee had walked out on him and gone off with another man. He was stunned and life had come to a stop for him. He was a good Catholic, he said, and couldn't understand why this had happened to him. He felt God had forgotten him.

I had no answer to his question "Why?" But I could assure him that God still cared about what had happened to him. As I left the cab, he stuck his head out of the window and said, "Thanks, lady. Thanks for listening."

Love involves us with those who have lost their way through some bondage such as drugs or alcoholism. We like to keep aloof from those around us whom we meet on the street and prefer not to become involved.

One morning, on my way to work, I stood on the curb waiting for the traffic light to change. I noticed a young woman, evidently under the influence of alcohol, clinging to the light post. She was having difficulty keeping her balance.

The light changed and I started crossing the street. I had taken only a few steps when I heard a thud in back of me. Looking around, I saw the woman flat on her face, unable to make it the rest of the way. Momentarily, I wanted to dodge the issue and leave her for someone else to care for. Then I turned back, dragged her up to her feet and together we staggered the rest of the way across the street, barely making the traffic signal change. Before leaving her, I asked if I could call a cab for her. She just looked at me and said, "Why did you stop to help me?" The only reply was "God loves you." As I walked away, the thought passed through my mind that this could have been me had I continued pursuing happiness on my own terms.

Love is taking time out of one's life to chat with a hippie and discover that she is really a human being after all, with the same needs others have. Love is an adventure in just helping others in the small ways and happenings in life.

Often loving is just being a good listener in depth. I rushed out of the office to lunch at a nearby restaurant. The waitress put me at a table for two and I proceeded to order. As there were some office problems to be resolved, I was not interested in interruptions. The waitress asked if I would mind sharing my table with someone for the restaurant was very busy. I assured her I didn't mind and paid little attention to the newcomer being seated across from me. That morning I had asked God to help me to be a channel of His love to someone that day. Although I didn't recognize it as such, He was about to answer this prayer.

The woman tried to open a conversation with these words, "It is a beautiful day, isn't it?" I glanced up and responded mechanically that it was and returned to my problems of the day.

However, my luncheon companion didn't give up easily and again she said, "What a beautiful day it is outside, but not inside." There was a catch in her voice that caught my attention this time.

God made me aware that this woman was trying to say something to me and I was not being sensitive to her and to her needs. Silently, I prayed for forgiveness for my own self-centeredness which kept me from hearing her. I looked up and answered, "Would you care to tell me about the 'inside' and why it is not beautiful?"

The tears started to fall as she told me of burying her husband the previous day and how life had come to a standstill for her. She was extremely lonely and didn't know what to do or where to turn for help. She had come a long distance to the city to escape this aching void, thinking a change of scene would help.

My heart responded to her for I, too, knew the loneliness of losing one I had loved. We talked of various possibilities and things that she could do that would help a little in filling the vacuum which had been left. I suggested involvement in the various needs of others through organizational work; that she find some friends in her church to share life with; but most of all, that she seek the love and friendship of God.

She admitted that she had lost faith in God somewhere back along the way as she and her husband relied on their own strength when they came up against hard times. Now she needed a strength outside herself and there was none. I assured her God had not lost her and was waiting at that very moment for her to renew a close relationship with Him which she had once known. She promised to think it over and left to catch her plane.

Our paths never crossed again and I never did know her name. Through this encounter I became more aware of what God meant by loving my neighbor as myself, even the strangers I meet along life's way.

Returning home from Boston by train once, I watched the people streaming into the cars looking for seats. As I glanced up, a long blonde-haired, mini-skirted college girl, with large daisies painted on her knees, flung herself into the train seat beside me. After a few moments of silence, she announced that it was mid-year vacation and she was just returning from a real "blast." We talked about this "blast" for a while, which consisted of a weekend of drinking, pot and sex.

Then our conversation drifted toward the future and I asked her what her plans were. She had no immediate plans in sight.

Our conversation kept going back to her weekend and I could see that something was deeply troubling her now that it was over. Finally she blurted out that now that the fun of the weekend was over, she was afraid of what might have happened. For all she knew, she might be pregnant and she didn't know what to do. She must have been extremely troubled to confide in a stranger.

I begged her to go home and confide in her parents as to what had happened on the weekend. From her conversation, I gathered that they were on fairly good terms. Reluctantly, she promised to do this. Then consternation gripped her again.

"How will I ever get through this situation, especially if I am pregnant?" she exclaimed. It seemed a good time to bring up the subject of God and what He could do for her. She had never been inside a church door since her christening and knew little or nothing about God. On this basis, I found it very easy to communicate with her. I could feel her interest from her questions.

She asked, "If I do decide to do something about knowing this God, what happens to my yesterdays? They are not too pure." I asured her that if she asked God, He would forgive her and that through His forgiveness it would be possible to put the past behind her and begin life anew, no matter how things turned out. She would find a courage not her own to face up to her responsibilities.

We parted at the next station. I gave her my phone number in case she wanted to get in touch or I could be of any help in any way. My thoughts kept going back to this young girl and many others like her, searching for happiness in every possible way and never really finding it to be lasting.

Although I was not brought up in a religious atmosphere, my mother was always very careful of the company we kept and sheltered us from the seamy side of life. God seemed to be spending much time rounding out my life for me in circles never before ventured and I certainly was learning a great deal from these lessons.

Walking out of the hospital door, having visited a friend, I started strolling down the street toward Broadway which was four blocks away. I hadn't gone far when a man started to chase me, yelling that he would fix me. I didn't wait around to find out and ran for a coffee shop on Broadway.

The smoky shop was fairly well filled with people,

and others turned to look at the man staring in. How I prayed that God would keep him out there. Just then, the woman next to me reached out and touched my arm, saying, "Don't worry, dearie, his kind never come in — too scared!"

The waitress threw a napkin down on the counter and asked for my order. Nothing was too appealing, so I settled for a greasy doughnut and a cup of coffee, hoping that by the time I finished the man outside would be gone.

Meanwhile I struck up a conversation with my neighbor on the next stool. She mentioned that business was poor that day and she had decided to come in for a bite to eat. I asked her what kind of business she worked at. At this the man next to her snickered aloud. I ignored him and turned to her for the answer. She looked at me in amazement and said, "Don't you know? I'm what you would call a prostitute."

My face turned several shades of red and about that time I decided it was best to go. I slid off the stool, paid my bill and started out the door, more than glad to get out of there. My new acquaintance called after me, "Wait a minute and I'll walk a ways with you. It's safer that way." Of this I wasn't too sure.

I sent up an SOS to God, asking Him to do something. He didn't seem to hear. We started out of the shop together, with the rest of the patrons staring after us. As we walked along I thought I might as well make the best of the situation.

I asked her how she came to get into this sort of

life and why did she want to keep on in it. She was very willing to talk about it. She had come from the Midwest, hoping to make a career in acting. She managed to get a few bit parts, then her luck changed. For a long time she was without work and had no money to meet her expenses. There was no one to turn to for help. Then she became ill and there seemed to be no way out of the financial situation. It was at this point she became acquainted with a friend and was introduced through her to a life of prostitution. She did very well financially and was at present out of debt and had saved quite a bit of money. She confessed that there were times she wished she could get out of it and start a new life somewhere and perhaps in time she would. Right now it looked hopeless.

I told her that it was not hopeless. There was always God and He could help her if she wanted Him to. She shook her head and said, "Not the mess that I am in." I assured her that God did love her as a person and that He would more than welcome her as His child. However, He would expect her to give up her present occupation.

We came to the street where I was to turn off and she turned to go on her way. My heart went out to her as I remembered reading when Jesus had taken time out to care about such a person as she in His day. I sent out a silent prayer for her.

A week later I was riding home from work on the bus and who should board it but my street-walker. She had spotted me and remembered me and started down the aisle to sit with me. She was evidently well-known in the neighborhood, and necks craned. I am sure many thought I must be a new recruit, and I began wishing I hadn't promised God to be a loving "neighbor."

We talked a bit and she wistfully said that she had been thinking about the conversation of last week but guessed that it was impossible to find God. Again I assured her that she held the key to make a new life come into being. The choice was hers and hers alone.

Her stop came up and as she arose to leave, I asked her to keep in touch if she changed her mind. In order to do this, I asked for her address. She grinned sardonically and replied, "Sorry, I don't give it out — only to clients." She walked off the bus into the night and I never saw her again.

That night I asked God's forgiveness for my pride and for my failure to help her. It was the first time that I had been close to the seamy side of life. God had gone to some length to show me that this woman was His creation and had become marred by sin. Some of the stuffiness was gone from me for, outside of the established circle of society, I had encountered need where help was most needed.

This is God's world and it is also my world. I will not pass this way again, but as I pass through, I feel that God expects me to leave some sort of imprint upon this world, even though I am only one.

CHAPTER TWENTY-ONE

Why Christianity?

Christianity is not a theory or speculation, but a life; not a philosophy of life, but a life and a living process.

— *Samuel Taylor Coleridge*

THIS QUESTION has been asked of me countless times. My one reason for becoming a Christian ten years ago was that there had been a vacuum in my life. Nothing seemed to bring any lasting satisfaction. Life had been without purpose and meaning. The years that have passed since the day of decision have been years of experiment and adventure. God has brought into my life real meaning which has made living worthwhile in the midst of all the problems that we, as humans, face.

Happiness was something which I had long sought in various ways. I had searched for it among the material things of the world, in pleasures and position, but happiness seemed always to elude me, was always just out of my reach. Then I met the Master and am finding that His way of life is the real and only life that can bring lasting happiness.

In the crucible of life's experiences, I had found no stability. The things which once seemed so secure and dependable became ruins. Now that the eternal God is involved in my life in a personal way, there are the stability and dependability which I need to overcome life's problems. This relationship with Him gives me courage to go forward.

Somehow Christ's supreme offer to me, the power to be no longer the helpless plaything of temptation, to be able to conquer more than to fail, to be able to be the master in my own life, challenged me. In accepting this offer, I am finding a power that is relevant to life situations which had been completely lacking in my previous way of life.

The fears that once held me in their grip no longer consume me. This liberation is a continuous process, not a one-time deal. God is helping me to be free of these fears and making it possible to invest myself completely in today. What a difference Christ's presence with us makes, both in the serenity of mind and the inner joy of the spirit.

God did not guarantee He would keep me from trouble, but did promise me courage to face it. This He has given time and again. Being a Christian does not leave me without burdens. But God has promised that my burdens need never crush me. I have found that in daily living, the Christian falls into the same courses as those of the non-Christian as far as troubles, problems, and heartaches are concerned. Christ's way does not evade the realities of life but enables a person to meet them head on. Troublesome things do happen to me that do not seem to make sense, and during these times I have often cried out, "God, where are You? Why can't You do something? Why did this happen?" There is only the silence — no answer.

There are no pat answers to these questions. But I am discovering that Christ gives me the power which makes me greater than anything that can happen to me. God doesn't lift me out of the intense battles but keeps me steady during the struggle. Through these hard places, where everyone walks a beaten path, I am no longer alone. There are two of us — God and I. What resources are mine, what creativity, what adequacy for every facet of life! My part is to accept them and let God work life's problems out with me.

There is a dimension to human personality that is not solely explainable on scientific evidence. We have a sort of loneliness, a cosmic loneliness, for which there is no fulfillment until we are welded into fellowship with God.

I am a Christian because, having tried other philosophies, I find Christ's way workable in the "now" of life. This way of life is not one to be lived in mysticism alone but is down-to-earth living in every circumstance I find myself. In daring to apply Christ's principles to situations and relationships, I am discovering that miracles can happen. This is a way of life in which many times I fail but I can find forgiveness for every failure. It is a way of life that will continue into eternity for I now believe in life after death.

I love Jesus of Nazareth, Son of the living God, and my belief in Him is deepened by the facts of my own experiences. He becomes more real to me as I relate to others and become caught up in the various experiments of life. These facts are unanswerable

169

and indisputable. No one can meet the Master and go his own way exactly as he came. This Stranger of Galilee has made a tremendous impact on my life and I will continue to follow Him into new and sometimes strange pathways.

As I look back upon that moment of turning, I realize that new life did indeed come into being. It was the beginning of the end of the lonely way. This new life brought the integration of a once-divided heart. The emptiness is gone. The fever of search and the restlessness are over. For the first time in my life, I am really living.

I believe in Jesus Christ. This is not merely an intellectual affirmation. It is a soul-trust in Him for time and eternity, for He came to show us what God is like and what life could be like lived under His direction.

> To every man there openeth
> A way, and ways, and a way.
> And the High Soul climbs the High Way,
> And the Low Soul gropes the Low.
> And in between on the misty flats
> The rest drift to and fro.
> But to every man there openeth
> A High Way and a Low,
> And every man decideth
> The way his soul shall go.
>
> JOHN OXENHAM

NNORE

rewarding reading...
from Cook

LIVING UNAFRAID. Do you have fears? Most people do——and this book tells about some who overcame their fears by applying an age-old truth: "Thou alone, O Lord, makest me to live unafraid." Read their stories . . . gain encouragement from their victories. By Dr. Charles W. Keysor, director of publications, Asbury College. .   86439——$1.25

PEBBLES OF TRUTH. Poems for all Christians, on topics of basic interest: the love of God . . . faith . . . repentance . . . forgiveness . . . salvation . . . obedience . . . fellowship . . . freedom . . . rejoicing . . . loyalty. By Dr. William S. Stoddard, pastor of Walnut Creek (Calif.) Presbyterian Church. Illustrated.   86371——$1.25

THEIR FINEST HOUR. Engrossing biographies of people whose dedication to Christ still inspires those who share their faith. Some names you will recognize . . . others, not. For instance: William A. "Devil Anse" Hatfield. His conversion ended the most publicized feud in America's history! Photos. By Charles Ludwig.   82917——$1.95

THE PROPHET OF WHEAT STREET by James W. English. In hard cover, it was the choice of six book clubs! English, former editor of Boys' Life, tells the story of William Borders, a southern black Northwestern graduate who returned to lead Atlanta's black church to revitalized faith, improved housing, new self-respect.   72678——$1.25

ALCOHOLISM by Pastor Paul. Encouragement for alcoholics, and all who are concerned about them——a pastor tells how God helped him beat the bottle. Although well educated and respected, the author found release not through his own efforts alone, but through the help of God . . . and those who offered their strength.   72629——$1.95

O CHRISTIAN! O JEW! by Paul Carlson. A member of Christians Concerned for Israel, Pastor Paul Carlson traces the progress of prophecy . . . from God's covenant with Abraham to the miracle of modern-day Israel. He presents a seldom-seen side of Jewish-Christian relations to help Christians better understand Jews.   75820——$1.95

LET'S SUCCEED WITH OUR TEENAGERS by Jay Kesler. An eminent authority, the president of Youth for Christ International, offers a new understanding of the age-old but desperately new problems even the happiest of families must face: coming of age, discipline and love, peer pressure, drugs, alcohol, tobacco, the Church. 72660—$1.25

BEFORE I WAKE. Are you ready to face death—your own death, or the death of a loved one? Both philosophical and practical, this book by Pastor Paul R. Carlson presents the Christian view of the nature and destiny of man, draws on doctors, psychologists, lawyers and morticians to help one face grief, make a will, arrange a funeral. 86454—$1.50

CHRISTIANS IN THE SHADOW OF THE KREMLIN by Anita and Peter Deyneka, Jr. Why can't the rulers of Russia banish faith? They've closed churches, taught atheism in the schools —yet a vital (if unorganized) church remains. How can it be? Come and learn as the authors talk with Russian students, workers, professional people. Photos. 82982—$1.50

THE EVIDENCE THAT CONVICTED AIDA SKRIPNIKOVA by Michael Bourdeaux. This book places its reader at the side of a young Russian girl on trial. She chooses imprisonment to the abandonment of faith in a story that challenges ALL Christians. (Bourdeaux is a worker at London's Center for Study of Religion and Communism.) 72652—$1.25

HOW SILENTLY, HOW SILENTLY. Joseph Bayly's modern-day fables and fantasies lead to spiritual discoveries: The wise computer's treatise on whether or not Man exists. The boy who arrives at college with shields of pure gold and returns home with shining shields that nobody recognizes as brass. The Israeli, in America at Christmas—who was he? 73304—$1.25

LOOK AT ME, PLEASE LOOK AT ME by Clark, Dahl, and Gonzenbach. Two church women tell about their work with the mentally retarded, how concern led them through fear and revulsion to acceptance and love—also to the discovery that often behind the facade of physical unloveliness waits a warm and responsive personality. 72595—$1.25

C

FAITH AT THE TOP by Wes Pippert. The author, a seasoned UPI reporter in Washington, D.C., takes us into the lives of 10 prominent men and women who dared to bring Christ along with them on their way to the top—like Sen. Mark Hatfield, pro football star Charley Harraway, former NBC-TV reporter Nina Herrmann.   75796—$1.50

INVISIBLE HALOS by David C. Cook III. As the largest publisher of non-denominational Sunday School materials reaches the 100-year mark, its president and editor-in-chief presents this inspiring series of vignettes: unlikely heroes, people he has met during his busy life who have served for him as models of Christianity in action.   77289—$1.50

WHAT ABOUT HOROSCOPES? by Joseph Bayly. Is there reality behind them? Can they really foretell the future? In giving the answers to these questions, the author examines not only astrology, but mediums (and the "spirit world"), Satanism, witches, possession by demons, ESP—the whole range of "in" occult topics.   51490—95¢

WHAT A WAY TO GO! by Bob Laurent. For adults . . . to pass along to young people! They'll like singer-evangelist Laurent's conversational style and understanding approach. Bringing new faith to thousands, he packs solid Christian advice under catchy labels like Saved, Satisfied, and Petrified . . . and Jesus Signed My Pardon.   72728—$1.25

CAMP DEVOTIONS by Dick and Yvonne Messner. Like Jesus, Christians can use the glories of nature as inspiring object lessons—on a mountain, during a sunrise, near a lake. Each short, one-subject devotional offers site suggestion, Scripture text, theme, and prayer. (Yvonne Messner is a camp founder and teacher of camping.)   75945—$1.95

CAMPFIRE COOKING by Yvonne Messner. Pack-along guidebook to fixing tasty, nutritious meals from scratch in the out-of-doors. What utensils are needed? What preparation and cooking methods should be used? Which recipes are best? How can a group get the most from its time and money? A camper tells you. Illustrated   75937—$1.95

D